GoodParents.com

GoodParents.com

*What every good parent should
know about the Internet*

ROBERT MAYNARD

Prometheus Books
59 John Glenn Drive
Amherst, New York 14228-2197

Published 2000 by Prometheus Books

Inquiries should be addressed to
Prometheus Books
59 John Glenn Drive
Amherst, New York 14228–2197
VOICE: 716–691–0133, ext. 207
FAX: 716–564–2711
WWW.PROMETHEUSBOOKS.COM

04 03 02 01 00   5 4 3 2 1

Library of Congress Cataloging-in-Publication Data

Maynard, Robert, 1962–
    GoodParents.com : what every good parent should know about the Internet /
Robert Maynard.
        p.   cm.
    Includes index.
    ISBN 1–57392–270–6 (pbk. : alk. paper)
    1. Internet (Computer network) and children—United States. 2. Computer
networks—Access control—United States. I. Title.
HQ784.I58M38   1998
025.04′083—dc21   98–36925
                                                                         CIP

Printed in the United States of America on acid-free paper

Contents

Introduction

I'VE HAD MANY TITLES IN my life: CEO of one of the largest Internet companies in America; commander of some of the most elite soldiers in the world; husband, son, and student, among others. All of these titles came with responsibility, rewards, and stress. But they all pale in comparison when it comes to the most important title I will ever hold: *Daddy*.

The day in 1991 when the nurse said, "Come here, Daddy, your daughter is hungry," I felt my knees go weak and the room spin. Of course, I had known intellectually that I was going to be a father, but hearing that word when she said it while holding my oldest daughter struck me deep in some primal core of consciousness. All at once I wanted to build a fire, grab a spear, and come back with fresh meat for the hearth. But, since it wasn't hunting season in Lake Havasu, and the hospital gift shop was fresh out of spears, I had to settle for a bottle of formula and a rocking chair. (My wife was recovering from complications of the delivery.) That's when I began to realize what responsibility really means.

Sure, I'd been responsible before. I'd even been responsible for the lives of other men before. So awesome a responsibility shouldn't have been anything new. But each time before, the responsibility had been temporary. I knew there would always be a time in the future that I would give up my responsibility, or I would at least be sharing it with someone else.

But here in my arms was a responsibility from which I would never be relieved. No one else in the world could or would ever be Daddy to my little girls. Every moment I lived, whether I was with them or ten thousand miles away, I would always be Daddy. I couldn't escape it, even if I wanted to. And I love it.

Well, if you've picked up this book, I'm not telling you anything new. Chances are you're a parent and you had your own little epiphany the first time you realized that you would always be a mom or a dad.

As you've probably realized, this is no ordinary computer book. To use this book, you don't need to know what http:// means or even how to work a computer. If the only kind of engine you know about is the kind that runs your car, and the only "Yahoo!" you know is the guy down the street who shoots his pistol every Fourth of July, then you'll be fine. This book will make you just enough of an expert to fool your kids into thinking that you know what you're talking about and that if they do bad things on their computer, you'll find out and then they're going to get it. If you've been using a computer for years and feel like you're competent, I'm willing to bet the price of the book that you will learn a thing or two that can help you, too.

This book is going to help you understand enough about the Internet so that you can guide your kids into a wondrous universe of information and people from around the world. It will also help you keep them out of trouble by knowing what to look for and how to keep them safe. I'm going to cover some very adult topics: sex, the human body, and George Carlin's seven dirty words, among other things. I will do this not to be crude, but to show you what's out there, how easy it is to find, and how to check if your children have been into it and other things that kids shouldn't be into.

You may not need to understand the Internet to do your job or advance in your career. But *your kids must be Internet literate* in order to succeed at virtually anything in the coming decades. The Internet is not a fad. It's here and it's already completely revolutionizing the way we communicate and receive, store, and distribute information about virtually everything.

You teach your kids to read, don't you? Well, keeping your kids off the Internet because you are concerned that they may run into people and places that might not be good for them is like not teaching them to read simply because one day they might pick up a copy of *Playboy* or *Penthouse Forum.*

I submit to you that your kids need to know how to find information and communicate on the Internet almost as much as they need to know how to read. In just a few years, there will be computers in cars that can access the Internet for directions, restaurant reservations, movie tickets, and e-mail. It's on the way, I've already seen the prototypes. And that's only the beginning. I don't think any of us can even imagine what's in store for us twenty or thirty years from now.

So relax. This book is easy. (See—it's not too thick and you only have to read half of it, since it includes instructions on two totally different pieces of software and you'll only be using one.) I don't use many big words. Besides, this material really isn't that hard, anyway.

We've included a CD for you that has all kinds of software and valuable savings engineered specifically for you and your family. Throughout the book I'll refer to different components of this software and show you how you and your kids can use it to solve computer problems that we all face.

If you don't have a computer, don't worry. You're going to learn a lot about how the Internet works and some of the great activities to do out there, so you can relate to your kids when they talk about what they did in school. You'll also learn how easy it is to get your kids pointed in the right direction on the Internet and keep them going that way. If and when it comes time for your family to buy a computer, you can call us at (800) Goodparents and we'll tell you which one we recommend.

So, what are you waiting for? Turn the page and let's get started.

Chapter One

——————————■——————————

So, How Does It Work?

"The Internet is a group of millions of computers linked together by a common (TCP/IP) protocol."

T HERE. CLEAR AS MUD, RIGHT? For those of you who are in the telecommunications or Internet business and actually understood that definition, please, by all means, skip this chapter and move on to the next. I'm probably not going to teach you much you don't already know. The other 99.99999 percent of us will spend this chapter getting a working knowledge of how this thing called the Internet operates.

So . . . how *does* it work? Short answer: Who cares! Do you know how the telephone system works? How your car works? How the water system works? Probably not. You just use it and expect it to work, right? The same goes for the Internet, but here are a few things to know so that your son or daughter will think you know what you're doing, and when something goes wrong you just might have an idea of which button to push.

Yes, the Internet is a massive bunch of computers around the world whose system administrators have agreed to link their computers together in a language they all understand. We'll call them *Geeks* from here on for lack of a better term, because *system administrator* is just too many letters to type over and over and I refuse to start cluttering up the book with acronyms. Anyway, the Geeks all agree to connect their computers together in order to share information and "transit" to other systems they want to talk to. . . . Okay, I see the glassy eyes already. Let's try it again.

When I was in college, I lived in a town called Flagstaff about two hours away from Phoenix, where my parents, and coincidentally, the parents of about 75 percent of the student body lived as well. The distance was great. No surprise visits, separate newspapers so that if we found our names in the police blotter our parents and their friends weren't likely to see it, and close enough to go home on the weekends and get the laundry done. But there was one little problem. Calling home was long-distance and, while collect was fine to check in and see how everyone was doing, it was really tacky to call collect when asking for money, which I found myself doing with great regularity.

By some serendipitous chance, I found that the phone in my dorm room was connected to a WATS line (you know, one of those lines that allows you to call a city long-distance without paying long-distance rates), which made calling Phoenix a free local call. Although I called home relatively often, I wasn't on the phone all the time. In fact, the phone was idle much more time than I was able to use it.

Now, imagine that someone else had the same kind of luck I had, except that his phone called Los Angeles instead of Phoenix. Well, if I ever needed to call LA, I could just make a deal with him to use his phone when he wasn't using it, and he could use mine when I wasn't calling Phoenix. It wouldn't cost any more to be neighborly, and I just might need to call LA once in awhile. Makes sense, doesn't it?

Congratulations. You've just con-
quered the most complicated concept on
the Internet today. The Geeks call what
I did in college *Peerage* or *Reciprocal
Transit.* They use words like this to convince everyone that what they are doing
is so complicated that mere mortals like
us could never possibly understand it.
But, truly, they're just making a deal
with someone who has the computer
equivalent of a WATS line going where
they would like to send some data.

Indeed, WATS stands for Wide Area Telephone Service. The Geeks
call it a WAN, or Wide Area Network, when it's computers, rather
than people, doing the talking.

Let's take a minute to expand this example and show you how this
might work in a larger situation. Suppose my friend with the LA connection had a much richer social life than I and he had set up this

kind of deal with lots of other people who had WATS lines to all sorts
of places. If we'd set up our original deal so that if he made an agreement with someone else to call, say, Chicago, then that deal would
extend to me as well. Now I can call Chicago for free anytime and the
guy from Chicago can call Phoenix whenever he has a mind to.

It didn't really work that way for me in college, but it does on the
Internet. This linking of "peered" computer systems around the
world is why it doesn't cost anything to look at computer data in, say,
France, while you're on the Internet from Topeka. Why, you ask,

would anyone want to talk to a computer in France? Well, how about taking a tour of the Louvre museum over the Internet?

"Museums, I hate museums," you respond scornfully. "Wouldn't catch me dead in one." Maybe that's true, but someday your kid is going to get an assignment to do a report on Impressionism. (That's a painting style and I only know because long ago I had to do a report on Impressionism myself.) When that day comes, the conversation will probably go something like this:

"Daddy?"

"Yes, honey."

"What's Impressionism?"

Here's where parenting gets tricky. Personally, I wanted my kids to think I was omniscient until they were at least sixteen. Unfortunately, that little fantasy was shattered by my five year old. "Dad," she said in her most condescending tone, "everyone makes mistakes, even you."

At this point in the relationship, you can either pull a W. C. Fields: "Go away kid, you bother me." Or, you could make something up: "Impressionism is what comedians do when they pretend to be someone famous, like Dana Carvey doing Ross Perot." Or, you could say what great parents around the world are saying: "Well, I could tell you, but why don't we see if we can find what the Internet has on the subject?"

Right now, I'm going to skip over how you would find resources on the Internet referring to Impressionism. Don't worry, I'll come back to how you actually find this information in the next chapter. For now, I'm just trying to show you how it works.

So, let's assume that you actually know that the Louvre museum (on the Internet it's now called the WebMuseum) has a great collection of Impressionist

art, and that you can find it on the Internet at: http://hkein.ie.cuhk.
hk/Education/Art/louvre/paint/theme/impressionnisme.html. (Don't
panic. You'll rarely have to type in an address, certainly not one like
that.)

All of a sudden there you are, with biographies on Monet and
Manet. You show your daughter that Van Gogh was a Post-Impressionist. You already knew that, of course. And you help her print out
a picture of *Impression,* Monet's first work that
gave the genre its name, to use as her cover
page. You show her how to cut and paste quotes
from the Web to lay into her paper, and she
looks at you with big round eyes and says, "Oh
Daddy, you are so smart!" And all is right with
the world.

Of course, up till now, sweat is trickling down your
back because you're wondering how in the world you
can be connecting to a computer in France without
racking up those big international long-distance
charges. After all, you couldn't call the Louvre on
the telephone, eventually get to someone who spoke
English, and ask them to fax or mail the material to
you without paying the big bucks. That is, of course,
if you could actually find
a Parisian who wanted to
help you. Well, I have one word for you:
Peerage.

Recall that I didn't have to pay to talk
to a phone in Phoenix or LA with my college-day wheeling and dealing. Your
Internet
Provider, whether it's America
Online or some little company with
two hundred customers, has made
arrangements with some other com-

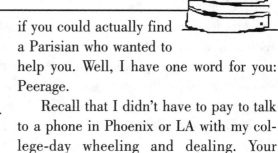

pany or university which has a WATS line to Paris, to use their connection when it's not too busy. And since computers communicate at light speed, it's not busy (idle, in Geek-speak) a lot.

When he opened for business, your Internet provider bought special computers called *routers* which keep track of who has a WATS line to where and routed you, in the blink of an eye, to the Louvre's collection of Impressionist art. You have achieved superhero status with your ten year old. You realize you won't need a second mortgage to pay the phone bill and, again, all is right with the world.

So, you see, the Internet works like a big community. Since communication is so easy through e-mail and the newsgroups (we'll get to them later), Geeks finding Geeks with links to other computers is relatively simple. And since they might someday want to talk to a computer that is connected to your computer, they (the Geeks, that is) agree to "Peer" with your Internet Provider, either because your Internet Provider has a bunch of customers, or he agrees to pay them, much like a wholesaler and retailer.

OKAY, SO WHAT'S THIS THING CALLED AN INTERNET PROVIDER?

Well, clearly, after the last discussion of Peerage, an Internet Provider is someone who has gone to the trouble and/or expense of setting up a bunch of peerage agreements around the Internet. The provider then usually expects to resell the time and money he has invested in putting the agreements together, along with the computers and people who run all of it, to people like you.

It really is pretty simple. For example, if I complained to you that I'd just bought the greatest phone; it was loaded with every option imaginable and did everything including toast bagels, but I couldn't get it to work, you would eventually get around to asking me if I'd ever bothered to contact the phone company to activate service. "Oh . . . ," I'd say, blushing brightly. "May I borrow your phone?"

Even if you have the greatest computer in the world, if you never call someone to give you "Data Dial Tone," you'll never get out of your house with it. Just like the phone company gives you voice dial tone and connects you to the global network of telephones, an Internet Provider connects you to the global network of computers called the Internet. Presently, the going rate for this kind of service is about $20 per month for a normal household, no matter how long you stay on the line.

So, how do you find an Internet Service Provider? (Those of us who like to pretend we know what we're talking about call them "ISPs.") At last count there are about four thousand ISPs in the United States and the quality of service they offer varies as wildly as their names. Regardless of who you use to access the Internet, the strategies and software I discuss in this book will work for you.

It's actually pretty straightforward nowadays. Preferably, you ask a friend who is on the Internet who he uses and you get a recommendation. If you don't have any friends, or the friends you have look at you with glassy eyes when you ask them who they use to get on the Internet, then simply look in the back of this book. We've included a CD with all the software you will need to connect automatically to the Internet. Depending upon where you live, you will connect to NetShield; Mindspring; or, if you'd prefer to walk before you run, America Online (AOL). It's obvious why I'm recommending NetShield—after all, my best friends and I built it. Mindspring is probably less obvious.

My wife and I started Internet America in an extra bedroom in our home in Dallas and built it into one of the largest Internet Providers in the country. We sold it a few years after starting it so that we could provide some freedom and security for our family and move back to our hometown.

Even while building that company, I had always been uncomfortable about some of the content available on the Internet, even through our own systems. Unfortunately at the time, there was no practical way to dynamically block content from the provider's side. About a year after selling Internet America, we decided that there was a need for an Internet Provider that simply did not allow the filth, smut, and hateful things I talk about throughout this book. Since no one else seemed to want to do it, some of my friends and I decided that we would. Thus, NetShield was born.

NetShield is definitely a PG-rated Internet service. We do not allow access to the more nefarious parts of the Internet through our systems at all, regardless of the age of the user in your home. So . . . if you want complete freedom on the Internet to see, read, and say anything you can imagine, you should go with Internet America, Mindspring, or any other company that meets the criteria I outline below. Most will give you great service at a fair price.

The techniques I show you in this book, combined with some active parenting on your part, and the CYBERsitter child-protection

software included on the CD in the back of the book, will make it safe for your kids to use the same computer as you. The software for Mindspring is also included on the CD in the back of this book and they will waive the activation fee when you sign up, saving you about thirty dollars. There, I've already given you a 150 percent return on your investment in this book!

If you want "kidsafe" access and you, the parent, aren't really interested in pornography, hate speech, or some of the more esoteric online activities, then simply install the NetShield software that is included on the CD in the back of the book. You still may want to install CYBERsitter software, but it's optional because the NetShield systems will very reliably prevent unintentional access to almost all reasonably objectionable content.

As much as they'd like you to think differently, AOL, Compu-Serve, and Prodigy do NOT supply you direct access to the Internet. These companies are big computer systems, called Bulletin Boards, that provide Internet access as an afterthought. In general they tend to be much slower than a direct Internet Service Provider, but AOL in particular does a great job in making things easy to use.

If you receive a recommendation for a local provider, and don't want to use the ones that I've recommended, here are some important questions (and the answers you should expect) when picking an ISP. Of course, each of the providers we recommend answers these questions the right way.

Q: How much does it cost?

A: It shouldn't be more than $20 or $25 per month with a nominal activation fee. Definitely, there should be no charges or limits to the number of hours you spend online, since the kids tend to use the Internet as a substitute for the TV, sleep, food, and things like that.

The last thing you want is a surprise charge to your credit card of several hundred dollars because of heavy use by the kids. Also, beware the "cheaper-than-it-should-be" price or long-term commitments. It costs real money to run an ISP the right way. You will definitely get what you pay for and woe unto you if you go for the cheapest deal in the area.

Q: What kind of software do I get?

A: They should give you the latest versions of the most popular software around. At the time I wrote this, that was Microsoft Explorer, followed by Net-Shield. I have included examples for both NetShield and Explorer in this book. You need only review the tricks I teach you for the package you and your family will be using.

Beware the provider who answers: "You can use whatever software you want." Chances are that getting it to work is going to be nightmarish for you and the kids. It could be so discouraging, in fact, that you probably won't go back to see what the Internet has to offer afterward.

Q: What hours can I call for help? (aka, Tech Support)

A: You should expect twenty-four-hour live service by now, no voice mail, short hold times (except when they are having system trouble), and a local or toll-free number so that when you are holding, you're not paying the phone company for the privilege.

Q: Do you have a generator in case the power goes out?

A: This may seem like a strange question, but reliability is what really separates the quality from fly-by-night providers in the ISP industry. In 1996, two of the largest ISPs in the world were off the air for nearly a day because the power was cut to their data centers and they had no generator backup. Internet Providers who are serious about reliable access will have generators and redundant power grids that will allow for indefinite independent power to keep everything running.

So, although you could ask much more detailed and technical questions, a simple yes to this one will tell you if you are dealing with a company that is serious about what it does. And since they all cost about the same, you might as well go with someone who is doing it right.

Now that you understand how it works and how to get on line, let's teach you just enough to be dangerous and fool the kids into thinking you might actually know what you're doing.

Chapter Two

Getting Connected

BEFORE YOU CAN DO MUCH of anything, you must get your computer connected to the Internet. This means you need to call an Internet Service Provider. Basically, you are going to trade him money for a user name and password to access his system, some software to make your computer work, and help from people who know what they are doing whenever you have a problem. Follow my instructions in the previous chapter to get connected to a good ISP, or insert the CD that comes with this book and we'll get you hooked up to the one we think is best in your area. We'll also save you some money while we're at it. Chapter 11 includes detailed instructions for installing the ISP software included.

Assuming you have done that, you are now ready for your first experience in the virtual world. Here are a few questions and their answers to help you get through this process as painlessly as possible.

Q: Do I have a computer?

A: I know that sounds pretty basic, but you'd be surprised. I remember the legend about the customer-support representative for a big computer company who took a call from an upset customer.

"ABC Computer support, may I help you?"

"You sure can. My cupholder is broken."

"I'm sorry, sir. Did you say your *cupholder* is broken?"

"That's right, this darned thing is broken and I've only had it for a few months."

Pondering the question, the technician then said, "Uh . . . I'm sorry, sir. Did you say your *cupholder* is broken?"

"That's right, sonny. What are you, deaf?"

"Uh, no sir. I'm just not familiar with that particular option on our computers. You did mean to call ABC Computer Company, didn't you?"

"That's right. Says right here on the case, ABC Computer."

"OK. Well, I'll help you if I can. Would you describe this cupholder to me please?"

"You know very well which cupholder. The one that's built-in. You push the little button and the tray slides out. I put my coffee on it. But now it won't slide back in."

About this time the technician realizes that the customer was describing the CD-ROM drive.

The point of the story, aside from the comic relief, is that you will never ask a question or run into a problem that your ISP hasn't seen. No question is too basic. So relax, computers are easy, and you *can* do it.

If your computer is more than three or four years old, it probably doesn't count. Although most Internet software will run on a computer as old as a 386 with only 4 megabytes of memory, it will be very slow and unstable. When you decide that you need a new computer in your home (or that you need more than one), call us at (800) GoodParents and we'll tell you which models and vendors we recommend at the time. Technology changes so quickly that anything we print here will be obsolete in just a 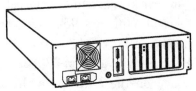 few weeks. If you have Internet access, go to the GoodParents home page at www.goodparents.com and you will find our reviews and recommendations there for free. If you don't have access to the Web, make the call. It could save you hundreds of dollars.

Q: DO I HAVE A MODEM?

A: Another basic question. If you're not sure whether you have a modem, turn your computer around so you can see the back where all the wires go. Search for a space that looks like a phone jack. Now here's where it might get a little tricky. If there is only one hole that looks like a jack, it's probably too big for a regular phone cord as well. That's not a modem, that's an ethernet card.

Your modem will most likely have two holes side by side which look like phone jacks. Look for the word "LINE." That's the one that connects to the wall. The other jack ("port" in computer language) will say "PHONE." You connect that one to a phone that you can use to talk on when you are not using your modem. Make sure that you plug the "LINE" port into the wall with a regular phone cord.

While you're searching for a place to plug the modem in, pick the whole computer up and move it into the kitchen, family room, or playroom, someplace where there is regular family foot traffic. One of the best ways to keep your kids out of trouble is to place them in an environment that will allow for unobtrusive oversight. If you put it in the kitchen, for instance, you weren't necessarily coming in to spy on them, you just wanted a snack, right? Of all the points we'll talk about in this book, that's probably the single best piece of advice I can give you to keep your children safe. Be where they are.

Now that you have the modem plugged in, turn on your computer. If it doesn't say "Windows 95" or "Windows 98," stop right now. Get your car keys, go to the closest computer or bookstore, and pick up a copy of Windows 95 or 98. There is a catch with Windows 98. It needs a relatively powerful computer to run, at least a 90-megahertz Pentium with at least 32 megabytes of memory and 200 megabytes of space on the hard drive. In other words, a pretty powerful home machine. If your computer is an older Pentium or 486, you may want to take it with you to the store and ask them to install as much memory as you can reasonably afford.

Speaking of upgrades (we were speaking of upgrades, you know), I do not recommend that you spend more than $250 upgrading your computer, including the license for Windows, which cost about $90 when I wrote this. The reason for this is quite simple. You can buy an entirely new computer with all the software and hardware you need for less than $600 and you won't have to go through the agony of an upgrade. When new computers cost $2,000 or more it made sense to deal with the pain of installing new hardware and operating systems. Now, the economics just don't work.

I'd recommend that you take your old computer down to your local elementary or high school and donate it. Now, I'm no tax advisor, but when I did this, I got to write off the original cost of my machine, about $2,500, as a charitable donation. In my tax bracket, that meant that I received a tax savings of about $850 on that year's return. In essence, I got a new computer with all the software and hardware I needed for the Internet, the school got a piece of hardware they really needed, and Uncle Sam paid for everything. Trust me, this is much easier than trying to upgrade your Operating System Software.

I know that there are other computer options, especially the Macintosh. But, in my opinion, Microsoft and Intel, Cyrix and AMD have passed Apple by for ease of use, stability, and performance on virtually every application that can be imagined for home use. The Mac itself is significantly more expensive than a comparable PC, and the software you can buy to run on it is limited and more expensive.

You've gotten your copy of Windows, and maybe a new computer. You've called your ISP and they've sent you the software, or you are using the software we sent you. Your computer is now located in the kitchen or family room. You've made sure that your modem is connected to the right port and is plugged into a live phone jack on the wall. Congratulations! You are now ready to surf.

Chapter Three

Connecting

W E'RE ABOUT TO GET OUT there and get on the Internet, that wonderful and terrible place that holds information to make you gasp in wonder. Like this picture of the Cygnus Loop, taken from the Hubble Space Telescope.

This amazing phenomenon, the remnants of an enormous supernova, is more than 100 million light-years away, three light-years

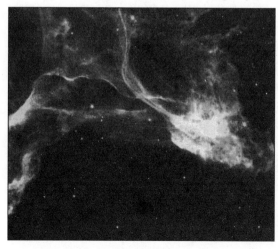

across, and moves at 3 million miles an hour, incinerating everything in its path at temperatures of more than 25 million degrees.

Or we can connect to hear the audio of John F. Kennedy's inaugural address, or footage from the first movie ever made, or

the contents of the Library of Congress and thousands of libraries around the world.

Or discussions between the greatest scientists alive today, or the millions of kids around the world learning how small this planet really is and how alike they really are as they talk to their e-pals from every corner of the globe.

All of this and countless more is free, once you have Internet access.

There is also stuff out there that will make you just plain gasp. Like the *Hustler* magazine Web site, or the newsgroups dedicated to the discussion of white supremacy and child pornography, or the live-sex video conferences.

There is some great software out there that can help restrict most age-inappropriate material from your computer. No software, however, can take the place of you taking an active role in your children's lives. However, while child protection software (which I discuss generally below and in detail in chapter 9) can be a great tool, it is not a cure-all.

In order to be most effective in keeping your kids safe and interested in learning, and still enforce your family's values, I believe you must be interested in what they're doing and have enough knowledge to guide them constructively in the virtual world.

Here are a few things that will help you get your family going.

- Show them that you have a clue when it comes to the Internet. Following my advice in this book is the fastest way to get there.

- Tell them what kind of behavior you expect and what they shouldn't do . . . a kind of family Acceptable Use Policy (AUP). You will find a suggested AUP later in this chapter.

- Move the computer into a common area.

- Police them from time to time and let them know you know how. That way they believe that if they're going to do something they shouldn't, the odds are very good that they are going to be caught.

- If your kids are under age seventeen, install CYBERsitter and keep it current. (*CYBERsitter is included on the CD* and discussed in detail in chapter 10.*)

- Give them some constructive, exciting places to go.

I believe the best child protection software is CYBERsitter. Written by Solid Oak Software in Santa Barbara, CYBERsitter is reliable, simple to use, and nearly impossible for the kids to get around. Better yet, unlike other programs with more name recognition like Cyberpatrol, the updates to the "off-limits" lists are made automatically and free of charge.

CYBERsitter integrates very sophisticated technology in a simple, easy-to-use in-

terface that runs all the time, without interfering with your system's performance or becoming overly intrusive. And, unlike most child-protection programs out there, CYBERsitter works with America Online (AOL).

We've included the CYBERsitter software and a free one-month trial on the CD in the back of this book. If you'd like me to help you install it, go to chapter 10 titled "Installing and Using CYBERsitter" and we'll do it together. No skipping ahead, though. You still need to read the rest of this book so you can have the basic understanding to help your kids when they need it.

But first, let's get your main Internet software installed and running. Each ISP treats things a bit differently, but it all works pretty

---

*CYBERsitter is being provided on the CD for the reader through a distribution agreement with Solid Oak Software.

much the same. If you want to use the CD we sent you in the book, turn to chapter 11 for detailed instructions on getting connected. Otherwise, follow your ISP's directions to install the software. By now, it's very straightforward.

I'm going to assume that you have either Netscape Navigator or Microsoft Explorer, and you are going to use one or the other for everything you need to do on the Internet. AOL Users can now use both Netscape and Explorer, but the vast majority use Microsoft's Explorer.

From this point on, I'll be giving you detailed instructions for both Navigator and Explorer. You need only review the sections that pertain to the particular software you will be using. When the procedures are different, I will let you know with a heading that says: Navigators Only with the Netscape Wheel   or Explorers Only with the Explorer Logo   .

I will also tell you the page number where the next section for you resumes. If the instructions are the same for both, I will let you know with the heading: Works for both Navigator   and Explorer   . This should save you a great deal of time while giving you all the information you need.

Navigators only   . Explorers   jump to page 36.

You will probably see your Netscape icon on the desktop, which is the main screen of your computer.

If you don't see Netscape, *and you're sure you have it installed*, let's create a couple of quick shortcuts so that you can get on the Net quickly any time you choose.

After you install the software your ISP sent, you will eventually run into a box that looks like this:

Highlight the Netscape icon by clicking on it one time with the left mouse button. Then click once on the right mouse button to see this:

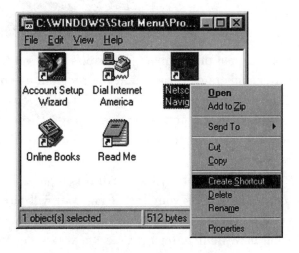

Highlight the "Create Shortcut" selection by pointing the mouse at the word. Click once on "Create Shortcut." You'll end up with another Netscape icon, this one saying "Netscape Navigator (2)." Click on this one time and hold the button down. While you're holding it, roll the mouse over to the blue-green part of the screen. You will now see this icon on the desktop (the blue-green part of the screen) every time you start your computer, making it easy to get to the Internet simply by clicking twice quickly (computer users call it a double-click) on the Communicator icon. The first time you do you will probably see this message:

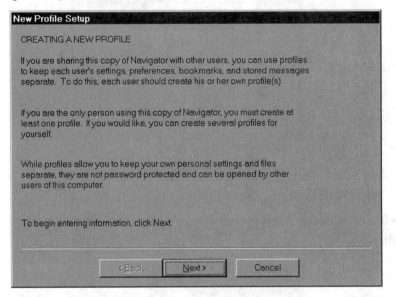

One of the great things about Netscape's latest version is that several family members can use it and the program is smart enough to keep all their settings separate. So you can all have your own e-mail address, bookmark list, and—you guessed it—History File! Oops, I forgot, we haven't covered that yet. So Click "Next" and we'll get started.

The directions are pretty clear. All this information should have been provided to you by your ISP. If not, you will have to call their support group to get the right settings. Don't worry about what all this means right now, we'll go over it in the next three chapters. By then you'll be an expert.

Let's set up your e-mail address first. Double-click on the Netscape icon. You should see

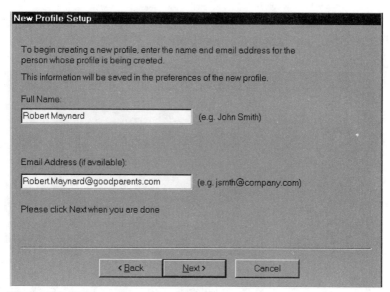

This screen is really easy. Unless there are two of you in the house with the same name, just click Next. If you're a Senior and your son is a Junior, then make sure you change the profile name so that there is no confusion. Click Next.

If all you see is the Netscape home page rather than the setup wizard, select Edit and Preferences like this and we'll quickly check to see if you're set up properly.

First, let's set up your default Home Page. Remember, you don't need to know what all this stuff means right now, you will soon enough. For now, just follow along blindly and trust that I'm not going to get you into trouble. I want you to set your default page to a site called "Yahooligans" which is a great place for you and your kids to launch your Internet Explorations.

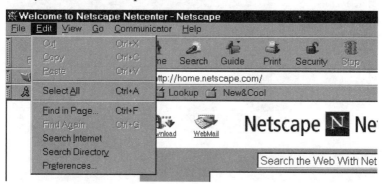

Your screen should look substantially like this. In the space for "Home Page" enter "www.yahooligans.com" (without the quotes) like I did below.

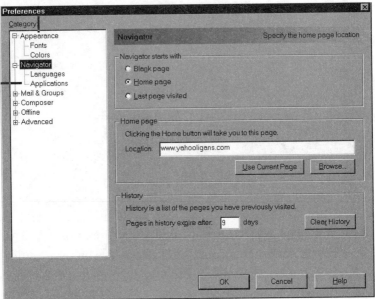

Now click on the little + sign next to the words "Mail & Groups" in the left-hand frame. And then highlight the "Identity" folder. Fill out your information like I did here.

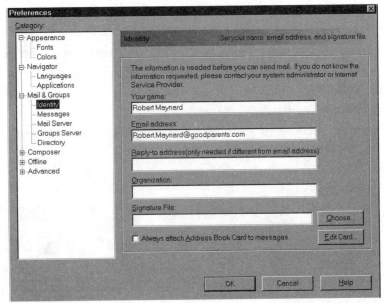

Next, click on the "Mail Server" folder in the left-hand frame and ensure that the information is correct for your ISP. If you don't have this information somewhere, you will have to contact your Internet Provider; don't assume that they are the same as I have written here.

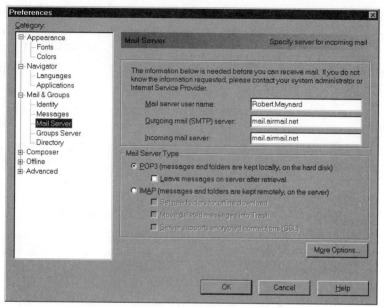

"SMTP" and "POP3" are two of the "Protocols" I mentioned earlier. You remember, the Geeks use fancy acronyms so they make us believe that there is some magic in what they do. In this case, the letters are pretty straightforward. SMTP is the Simple Mail Transport Protocol and POP3 is the Post Office Protocol, revision 3. Of course, you don't really need to know any of this, except to impress your kids and perhaps troubleshoot a problem if you have trouble sending or receiving e-mail.

The thing that you need to worry about is that you input the name of the server(s) precisely as your ISP has given them to you. Remember, everything here is CaSe SenSITiVe. If it's all lowercase, then you need to enter all lowercase letters; if all capitals, then you need to enter that. In short, you need to pay attention because to this kind of computer "A" and "a" are different. So, enter the name of your ISP's SMTP server here. Then click Next.

Enter the name of your ISP's POP mail server (aka their

"incoming" mail server). Make sure that you've selected POP3 as the Mail Server Type. IMAP is a new mail standard that will become more prominent in 2000 and later. For now, an IMAP server is extremely rare and you will know if you have one.

Finally, select the "Groups" folder in the left frame. I discuss Newsgroups in detail in another chapter. But, personally, I don't think there is really any legitimate reason for kids or casual adult users of the Internet to access Internet News. It's too untamed, wild, and dangerous. But, if you insist on using it, enter the name of your ISP's news server here, ignore the Port entry, and click Finish or OK, whichever is showing.

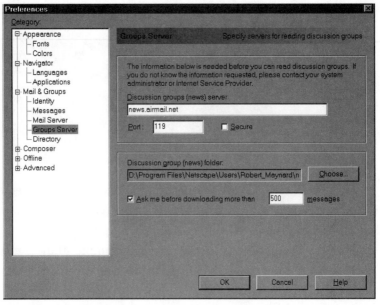

Explorers only  . Navigators go to page 37.

Creating a shortcut to Explorer is easy because it's already there. Much to the consternation of the U.S. Justice Department, every copy of Windows 95 comes with Explorer already installed and on the desktop. To start it, simply double-click on the 𝒆 . If you use America Online, then you will see the AOL logo ▲ .

Just one more step to take before you actually get on the Internet. Sit down with your kids and talk to them about what they are allowed to view and how they are to behave on the Internet. This is called the Family Acceptable Use Policy.

1. Tell them not to give out their name, address, or home phone number without checking with you first. (CYBERsitter will enforce this, requiring you to give permission before they can send that information.)
2. Tell them that they shouldn't go anywhere or do anything on the Internet that they don't want you to know about, because you *will* find out.
3. Tell them that they are not allowed to buy anything without asking you first. (Again, with CYBERsitter installed, you will restrict them from this as well.)
4. You will probably want to set some guidelines for use, like maximum time or the specific range of hours they can spend on line every day, or homework, chores, and exercise completed before going online.
5. You will want to add those issues specific to your family. For instance: "We do not allow pornography in our home, don't put it on your computer because I WILL find out."
6. Finally, you need to talk to them about their abuse of other people and computers on the Internet. This is such an important issue that I have devoted the whole of chapter 8 to it.

Double-click on the Netscape Navigator shortcut we just created and left on the desktop or the Explorer icon *e* that's already there. Although Windows 98 and Windows 95 both look a bit different, they are close enough that whichever program you are running, everything will look much the same. Anyway, whenever you try to do something that requires Internet access, Windows modem dialer, called Dial Up Networking, will fire up and ask you the following:

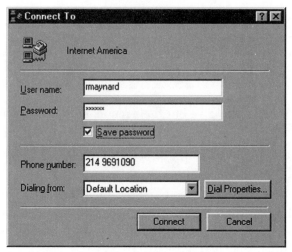

Input the password supplied by your ISP. Be careful, since these things can be finicky. Unlike most of the computers you may have used, the Internet is usually CaSe SenSItive, especially here. Thus, the password will be different if you type "PaSSword" or "password." So, very carefully type in your password exactly as it was given to you, and then hit the "Connect" button.

At this point you should hear your modem start dialing your ISP. Eventually, you will see the box change into these three different combinations.

The first time people try to launch this, they often get an error that says: "No Dial Tone." This usually means that you have not plugged the phone line into the correct port on the modem, or that there is no dial tone in the jack on the wall. To test the wall jack, take any ordinary phone in the house and plug it in. If you hear a dial tone, you're okay. Make sure that the phone cord is plugged into the port that says "Line" on the modem.

You will then hear the modems squealing at each other (that's called handshaking) and in a few seconds, you should see:

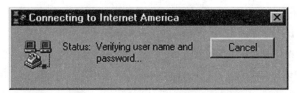

At this point, you may encounter an error that says you have been disconnected. This is likely a result of misspelling or incorrect case for either your username or password. To quickly troubleshoot the problem, close your browser by clicking on the little "X" in the top right corner, and then restart it with a double-click. Take great care to reenter the information perfectly.

Then, assuming you've correctly input the password and dialed the right number, voila! You are connected to the Internet!

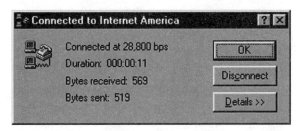

If you have a 28.8 or faster modem, you may notice that you do not connect at the maximum rate that your modem is capable of. This is a result of the quality of the phone lines between your modem and the modems at your ISP, which may slow down your activity on the Net. Check to make sure that you don't have a cordless phone attached to the same phone line in that room, and that the cord between your modem and the wall is not more than ten or fifteen feet. Other than that, there's not much you can do about it other than hope that your local phone company updates its system soon. There is little, if anything, that your ISP can do about it.

If you have any trouble connecting that I haven't covered, it's time to call your ISP for help. This is where your ISP will show his true value. If you're using one of the ISPs we've recommended, they will be there twenty-four hours a day, every day, to help diagnose and fix any problem you may have.

Now, minimize this window by pushing on the little "_" on the top-right-hand corner of the box. *Make sure you don't click on the "X"; that will terminate your connection.*

Congratulations! You are now on the Internet. When you get done celebrating, move on to the next chapter and I'll show you how to start using it.

Chapter Four

Surfing and Searching the Web

T
HE INTERNET HAS GAINED WIDESPREAD popularity on the strength of the World Wide Web. That's the graphic point-and-click environment that makes getting around simple and intuitive. It's just great for kids.

Your browser should now be open. If not, open it by double-clicking the left mouse button and Netscape or Explorer will launch to whatever home page has been set up as its default, probably the home page of your ISP.

Predictably, mine loads up to my ISP, and, while it's a great site, it's not the best one for your kids to start from. So, let me steer you straight to a site that is devoted to nothing but searching for things on the Internet. Take the mouse and point on the address that is currently shown in the location box. In this example, it's http://www.air-mail.net. When using Netscape, it will look like this:

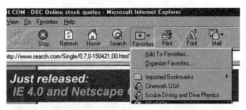

For Explorer, it will look like this:

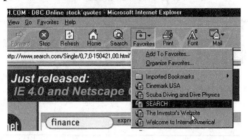

In either program, just click once on the letters "http://". You'll see that the whole block is highlighted in blue. Without doing anything else, type in www.search.com (exactly) and hit the Enter key. You should have automatically erased what was already there and in a few seconds, you will see the new site start to come up.

You are now at a computer in California that is dedicated to helping you find your way around the Internet. Remember when we went to the Louvre museum and found Impressionist art? Let's do that search so you can find it yourself.

No one knows exactly what is on the Internet. On any given day, more than two thousand new sites appear, so even keeping up with a week's worth of content would take most normal people years to explore. So the Geeks have developed computers called "search engines" whose only task is to constantly troll the Internet and catalog new content as it appears.

Now there are more than fifty different search engines and they all compete with each other for the bragging rights about who is the best on the Internet. Search.com is a search engine for search engines, constantly rating and updating the best ones, which is why I've sent you there.

Remember when I told you that I would give you some easy secrets that would convince your kids that you actually know what you're doing out there? Well, here's one:

When you get to search.com, scroll down the screen by clicking and holding the little down button in the lower right-hand corner of the screen until you see the "Express Search" area of the page.

Your conversation should go something like this:

"Let's go down to the Express Search area and use Lycos. I think it's the best search engine out there right now and much better for finding information like this."

Your kid, who had no idea you were so smart, looks at you with a mixture of awe and terror as he realizes that you might actually know how the computer works. That means you might be able to figure out what he's been doing out there. Well, that is the point of the illusion now, isn't it?

"Okay son, in the space, type 'Impressionism' and select Lycos as your search engine. Then press the 'Search' button."

And, in a couple of seconds, there it is. The link to the WebMuseum's Impressionist section. "Ah, there it is, right where I thought it would be. Go ahead and click on it" you say with great confidence.

With the push of that button, you have now left the search.com computer in California and have been transported halfway around the world to Paris and the Louvre's digital collection.

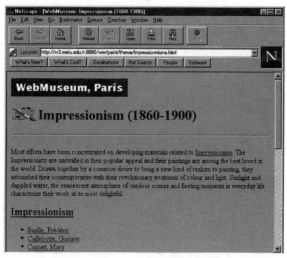

"Okay," your son says, "now what?" And you think to yourself, Uh-oh, the jig is up.

Don't panic. See the underlined words? Each of these is called a "hyperlink." That means there is more information underneath it.

Keep your bearing and say, "Well, push the link that says 'Impressionism.' " (By the way, you may not know it, but you have been surfing the Web for some time now. Not really that hard is it?)

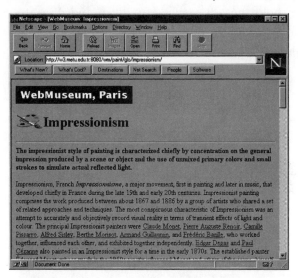

Now you have a professionally written history of Impressionism, including a list of the more influential artists of the genre, as well as links to their work. See the link for Claude Monet? If you just click on it . . .

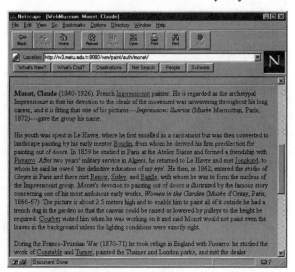

You find his biography, an analysis of his work, and even samples of his painting. If you have a printer, you can choose to print the whole page by selecting File and then Print with your mouse. But better yet, you can incorporate passages without having to retype them. Simply point the mouse at the place where you want to start the quote, then hold the left mouse key down and drag it over the part you want to copy. After you have selected the quote you want, select Edit and then Copy from the menu like so:

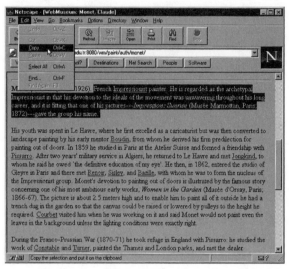

And then paste it into the word processor you are using for the report by selecting Edit and then Paste. And in no time we have the start of a great report:

"According to the Louvre museum in Paris, Claude Monet 'is regarded as the archetypal Impressionist in that his devotion to the ideals of the movement was unwavering throughout his long career, and it is fitting that one of his pictures—Impression: Sunrise (Musée Marmottan, Paris; 1872) —gave the group his name.' "

And if that weren't enough, with moderate graphics capabilities, you can even add the picture that got it all started: *Impression.*

Now how does that report look? The kid's an "A" student!

There's really not much more to searching than just typing in a word or two in the right place and using the best search engines out there. Again, I took you to search.com because it seems to be committed to finding the latest in searching technology and getting it out on the Internet.

Now for something that's not so great about the Internet—at least as far as kids are concerned. You can do a search for "sex" just as easily as Impressionism. And the computers are just as effective. It's probably a sad commentary on the human condition that "sex" was the most often searched-for term on the Internet in 1995, 1996, 1997, and 1998. But thankfully, that's changing quickly as we begin to realize the valuable uses of the Internet as a learning and communications tool, rather than a hi-tech pornographic magazine.

So, allow me to take you back to search.com and I'll show you how serious the issue is.

Without your kids at the computer, go back to SEARCH.COM. Scroll back down to the Express Search area we went to for the Louvre. Type in "sex" (without quotation marks) and select Lycos as your search engine. Here's what I got in about three seconds.

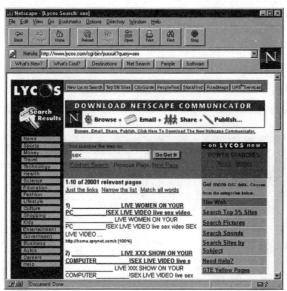

Not only are there 6,001 links relating to sex, the first one is a virtual strip bar where women will strip in front of their computer and you can watch it in the comfort of your home or office. The artificial intelligence that makes Lycos so smart is actually working overtime here. Notice that the ad banner across the top is a sex-related ad. And the page has even told you that there are more sites available and eagerly offers to help you index them by category. Lycos has no way of telling if you are an adult or a ten-year-old sitting at the computer; the machine is merely doing what it is asked.

Now we can rail all day long that this is bad and shouldn't be allowed. But it won't help. Even if we are successful in making this sort of thing illegal in the United States, we won't be able to ban it on the Internet. The technology is simply too powerful.

Remember when we connected to the Louvre in France? Well, in France, prostitution is legal. I've been to France. The ads on the bus stops are so racy that you wouldn't need to buy *Playboy* if that was what got you going. Is France going to outlaw this kind of material on the Internet on the chance that your child is going to see it? Not likely. And even if France does, will Thailand? Greece? the Philippines? You get the point. It takes less than two seconds for data to travel around the world. We need to deal with the fact that we are not going to be able to control what's out there.

If you have installed CYBERsitter, or the NetShield Internet Service as I recommend, your computer will know you don't want this material in your house and will tell the search engine. In that case, a search for "sex" on the same site with CYBERsitter or NetShield running will return nothing at all—a blank page.

Navigators only 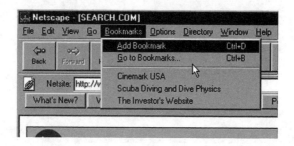 *. Explorers* 🄔 *resume on page 54.*

Since it looks as if we'll be going to search.com often, let's make a bookmark.

In the address window of Netscape, type in www.search.com again and hit the enter key. Once you get there, click on the "Bookmarks" button on the top left and click on "Add Bookmark."

Netscape automatically adds the bookmark for you so that the next time you want to go to search.com, you can just click on Bookmarks and then highlight the SEARCH.COM selection that now appears. And you go straight there, with no more typing the address required.

Teach this trick to your kids. Not only will it continue to impress them as to your Internet skills, you can also learn a great deal about where your kids are going simply by reviewing the bookmark list from time to time. As you can see from the list above, my family likes to go check the movie times at our local Cinemark theater, as well as get information about SCUBA trips and our investment portfolio.

When you check the bookmark list, you can see the sites your kids like to return to or find interesting. Most people don't even think about the trail they leave here. Bookmarks are a great way to unobtrusively watch what your kids have been viewing.

Since we're talking about ways to figure out where the kids are going on the Internet, here's the one that will get them every time. Make sure they're in bed or at school, then, with Netscape open, go to the address window (where it usually says something like http://www.whatever.com), and type this: about:global.

What you will find is a list of every place that anyone using that computer has gone in the past sixty days, starting with sixty days ago and going down to the most recent, along with the date and time that the reader was there. A quick review should highlight anything fishy, since Web sites, especially pornographic sites, tend to have pretty descriptive names.

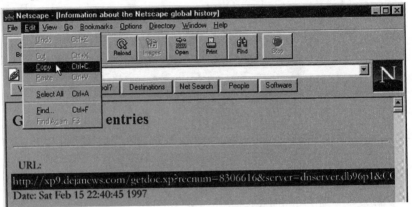

Here you see that I've been to, among other places, my company's home page, the home page for a company called Adobe, and Netscape's home page. As you scroll through the history, anything really blatant, like http://www.sexzilla.com or http://www.xxx.com, will likely jump right out at you.

CYBERsitter, once installed, will go one better and actually show you all the attempts at inappropriate places, who tried to go there and when, and lots of other information. I'll go over this powerful tool in chapter 11. If you see a site that you're not sure of, just click on it and Netscape will launch to it.

Check the history file about a week after you've had the Internet in the house, then every few weeks thereafter. After you've visited a few of their favorite places, have the following conversation at the dinner table, especially if your children are teenagers.

"I see you like that (insert one of the places they go, in my example it's the dejanews.com) site. What do you like the most about it?" Casually take another bite of meat loaf and enjoy the confused look on their faces.

They'll respond as calmly as they can with "Um, it's always really fast." Or some other equally lame answer. Their minds will, of course, be screaming, "How does she know that?"

"That's nice. I thought it was pretty cool myself." And your point is made. Enforcement of the talk you had earlier about the house rules should be a snap from now on.

Although this history file can be defeated, it's pretty hard. If your kids have figured out how to do it, it will show up blank or extremely short, another red flag. As far as I know, there is no way to edit it or erase one entry. If your kids figure that out, forget it, you'll never catch them anyway.

Now that you know about some of the bad stuff and how to catch your kids in the act of viewing it, let's do something more productive.

Here's a great site for your kids. It's called "Yahooligans."* Yahoo is a company that specializes in search engines for the Internet. Yahooligans is the version they built just for kids.

The entire Yahooligans site is designed to help parents and their children make the Internet easy to maneuver and hard to get into trouble. For instance, if I search for "sex" on the Yahooligans site, I get the following message:

No match found for **sex**.

Try searching for another word, or explore the Yahooligans! categories. You'll get closer to what you are looking for with every click!

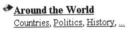

Around the World
Countries, Politics, History, ...

School Bell
Clubs, Homework, Math, ...

Art Soup
Books, Dramas, Dance, ...

Science & Oddities
Space, Animals, Robots, ...

So Yahooligans is definitely PG rated. Unfortunately, it comes up with the same answer (no sites found) if you search for Impressionism as we did in the previous example. Its intelligence isn't well suited for single-word subjective searches like that.

Yahooligans is better when you are looking for categories or specific places, Lycos is better for general topics. However, if we had known that the Louvre had a great collection of Impressionist paintings, we could have searched simply for the Louvre and found it that way.

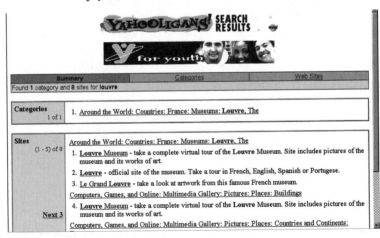

Since your kids will be using the Internet more every day, my advice is to set your version of Netscape up to always open on the

Yahooligans home page. That way your kids can start exploring in an environment that is not going to hurt them. Here's how you do it:

Open Netscape by double-clicking the left mouse button on the "N" icon that we built on the desktop. Once you see that Netscape is open, go to www.yahooligans.com by typing the address into the address bar. Click on the word "Edit" across the top. Then click on "Preferences" like this:

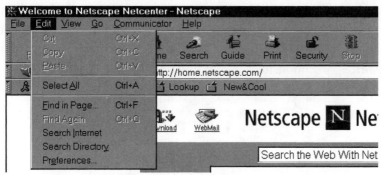

Since you should already be at Yahooligans, push the button in the middle that says "Use Current Page" and then "OK." Now, every time you or your kids start up Netscape, it will always open to Yahooligans, a safe portal for everyone in your family to launch their exploration of the Internet.

If you still haven't done it, move the computer out of the back bedroom and into the kitchen, family room, or den, some common area where you have a right to walk in unannounced. This will keep most of the nonsense from even starting. Again, it's one of the most effective things you can do to enforce your family's values and keep your kids out of trouble.

The science of searching is always evolving, so don't be afraid to click on the "help" and "advanced search" links at any of the search sites to give yourself great tips on using the search engines to give you the most fruitful response. Back when we did the Louvre search, it really was kind of lucky that the first link in our search was to the exact site we wanted.

But kids are sponges. They'll figure all of this out on their own if we just give them a boost. And you've given them plenty of encouragement, as well as taking steps to protect them from themselves. Now get out of the way and let 'em at it.

This is the longest and most complicated chapter. You've done a great job so far. Take a break. When you come back, we'll get started on e-mail (go to the beginning of chapter 5 on page 63).

Explorers only . **Navigators** **go to page 63.**

Since it looks as if we'll be going to Search.com often, let's make it a favorite. In the address window of Explorer, type in www.search.com again and hit the enter key. Once you get there, click on the "Favorites" menu at the top and click on "Add to Favorites."

Explorer then asks you if the name it has selected is okay with you. Always answer OK. You will see that it also asks if you are interested in "Subscribing" to this page. When you subscribe, you are asking the computer to notify you that the page has changed. You will usually want to select No here.

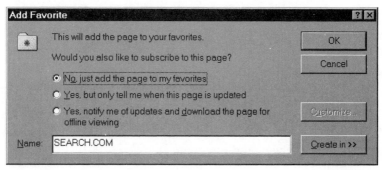

Explorer then automatically adds the site for you so that the next time you want to go to Search.com, you can just click on Favorites and then highlight the SEARCH selection that now appears. And you go straight there. No more typing the address is required.

Teach this trick to your kids. Not only will it continue to impress them as to your Internet skills, you can also learn a great deal about where your kids are going simply by reviewing the Favorites list from time to time. As you can see from the list above, my family likes to go check the movie times at our local Cinemark theater, as well as get information about scuba trips and our investment portfolio.

When you check the Favorites list, you can see the sites your kids like to return to or find interesting. Most people don't even think about the trail they leave here. And, once a Favorite is made, it's very difficult to erase. Keeping track of Favorites is a great way to unobtrusively monitor what they've been doing.

The latest versions of Explorer have an even easier way of adding a shortcut to the search function. They have added a "Search" button to the toolbar, right next to the "Favorites" button. When you click on "Search," a new frame opens on the left-hand side. Now the Search button looks like it's sinking into the toolbar and the frame on the left has a place for you to enter your Search query. To turn off this frame, just click again on the Search button and it will turn off.

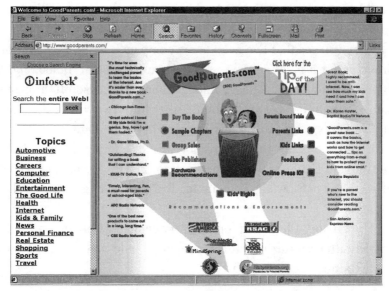

Since we're talking about ways to figure out where the kids are going on the internet, here's the one that will get them every time. Make sure they're in bed or at school, then, with Explorer open, select the "History" button on the main toolbar.

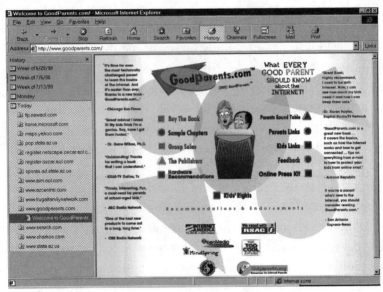

What you will find is a list of every place that anyone using that computer has gone in the past four weeks, listed alphabetically, along with the date and time that the reader was there. A quick review should highlight anything fishy, since Web sites, especially pornographic sites, tend to have pretty descriptive names.

Here you see that I've been to my company's home page, a caterer I'm using for a meeting next week, a map service at Yahoo, and the State of Arizona's home page, among others. As you scroll through the history, anything really blatant, like http://www.sexzilla.com or http://www.xxx.com, will likely jump right out at you.

If you see a site that you're not sure of, simply double-click on the title and Explorer will launch you to the site so you can see what little Johnny or Suzy has been up to. Truly, knowledge *is* power. Don't you agree?

The History file in Explorer is very easy to delete or manipulate. CYBERsitter captures all this information, and much more. More on CYBERsitter in chapter 10.

Check the history file about a week after you've had the Internet in the house, then every few weeks thereafter. After you've visited a few of their favorite places, have the following conversation at the dinner table, especially if they are teenagers.

"I see you like that (insert one of the places they go; in my example it's the State of Arizona) site. What do you like the most about it?" Casually take another bite of meat loaf and enjoy the confused look you are getting.

They'll respond as calmly as they can with "Um, it's always really fast." Or some other equally lame answer. Their minds will, of course, be screaming "How does she know that?"

"That's nice. I thought it was pretty cool myself." And your point is made. Enforcement of the talk you had earlier about the house rules should be a snap from now on.

Here's a great site for your kids. It's called "Yahooligans." Yahoo! is a company that specializes in search engines for the Internet. Yahooligans is the version they built for kids only.

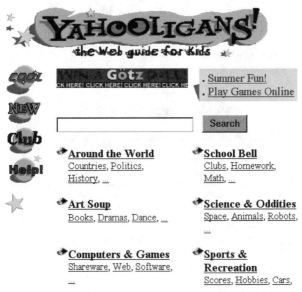

The entire Yahooligans site is designed to help parents and their kids make the Internet easy to maneuver and hard to get into trouble. For instance, if I search for "sex" on the Yahooligans site, I get the following message:

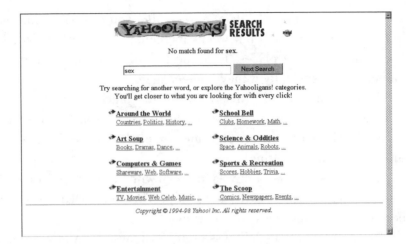

So Yahooligans is definitely PG rated. Unfortunately, it comes up with the same answer (no sites found) if you search for Impressionism as we did in the previous example. Its intelligence isn't well suited for single-word subjective searches like that.

Yahooligans is better when you are looking for categories or specific places rather than general topics like Lycos is. However, if we had known that the Louvre had a great collection of Impressionist paintings, we could have searched simply for the Louvre and found our way there that way.

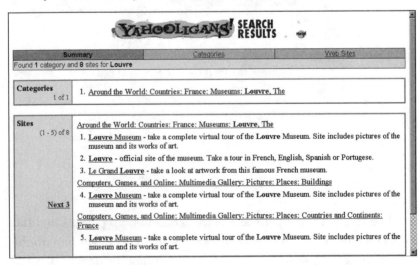

Since your kids will be using the Internet more every day, my advice is to set up your version of Explorer to always open on the Yahooligans home page. That way your kids can start exploring in an environment that is not going to hurt them. If you use the software we've included in the enclosed CD, this is already done for you. If you've got your own software, here's how you do it:

Open Explorer by double-clicking the left mouse button on the 𝑒 on the desktop. Once you see that Explorer is open, in the address bar type www.yahooligans.com. Once you get there, click on the word "View" and then "Options."

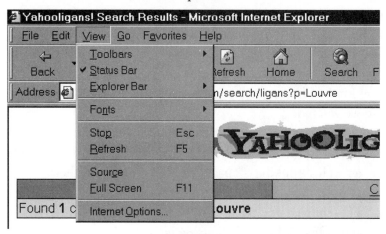

You should see this screen:

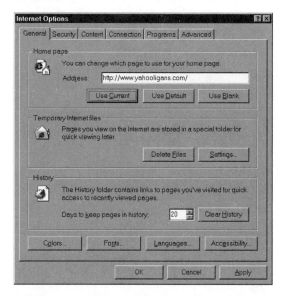

With your browser at www.yahooligans.com, click on the button that says "Use Current," then click "OK." Now every time your kids open Explorer, they will always open with the Yahooligans page. This is a great way to start their exploration of the Internet.

If you still haven't done it. Move the computer out of the back bedroom and into the kitchen, family room, or den, some common area where you have a right to walk in unannounced. This will keep most of the nonsense from even starting. It's one of the most effective things you can do to enforce your family's values and keep your kids out of trouble.

The science of searching is always evolving, so don't be afraid to click on the "help" and "advanced search" links at any of the search sites to give yourself great tips on using the computers to give you the most fruitful responses. Back when we did the Louvre search, it really was kind of lucky that the first link in our search was to the exact site we wanted.

But kids are sponges. They'll figure all of this out on their own if we just give them a boost. And you've given them plenty of encouragement, as well as taking steps to protect them from themselves. Now get out of the way and let 'em at it.

This is the longest and most complicated chapter. You've done a great job so far. Take a break. When you come back, we'll get started on e-mail.

Chapter Five

E-mail

SURE THE INTERNET IS AWASH in great sites; it's filled with more information than you can ever imagine, or use. But that's not what keeps it growing and strong. Ultimately, the Internet is about *communication*. The simplest and most widely used form of Internet communication is e-mail.

You probably know what e-mail is: electronic messages that you send back and forth over the Internet. They can be simple text, or they can have files attached (think of them as enclosures in a letter). As the software has become more sophisticated and transfer speeds get faster, you are now able to send embedded audio and graphics, and eventually video in your e-mail. Soon you will be able to include video.

THE GOOD STUFF ABOUT E-MAIL

I think that the single greatest thing about e-mail is that it is resurrecting the lost art of letter writing. Many of us lost the ability to express ourselves in writing because television, radio, and the telephone made written communication superfluous. That's hurt many of us, especially in our careers.

Many of the people I have worked with who are otherwise bright, motivated, ambitious people look like they just became unbearably motion sick when I ask for a one- or two-page memo on something they fully understand. At work, my insistence on e-mail communication forced many of them to hone their writing skills. Those who won't, or can't, express themselves clearly in writing have extremely limited opportunities in my companies. Imagine the benefit to your kids who will never know anything but written self-expression.

The next great thing about e-mail is that it provides a very intimate level of communication. This can be both good and bad, since it's very easy to be misunderstood, primarily because e-mail messages tend to be less formal than other types of writing. E-mail is quick, almost terse, in its structure. But it's like whispering in someone's ear, or talking over a cup of coffee—extremely effective and powerful. My father and I, distant and somewhat estranged nearly all my life, have grown much closer through our regular e-mail exchanges.

Importantly, Internet e-mail is dropping artificial boundaries and prejudices left and right. As your kids meet and greet people on the Internet, they'll begin to set up a list of pen pals (called e-pals on the Internet) with whom they will regularly correspond. Not once have I ever had or seen anyone ask something like "What color is your skin?" or "How big is your house?" You'll find that your kids start judging people they meet on the Net based on things like their spelling, grammar, and understanding of the technical intricacies of the subject matter at hand, rather than their skin color, appearance, or social status.

THE BAD STUFF ABOUT E-MAIL

You can't get into too much trouble with e-mail. About the worst thing that can happen is that someone gets hold of your e-mail address and floods you with lots of unwanted messages, or you may receive solic-itations for products or services you are not interested in. Once in a very great while I have seen people harassed through e-mail, rather like telephone harassment. In the unlikely event that you find that happening to you, turn to chapter 8, titled "Net Abuse," to see what you can do about it.

One important rule of the road with e-mail is that your kids never, ever give out personal information like your home address, telephone number, school, or credit card numbers. Make sure that you tell them they need your permission before they can send this to anyone. If you have installed CYBERsitter, I will help you set it up so that they must have your permission before they can transmit this data.

Making E-mail Work

Navigators ▨ *only. Explorers* 𝑒 *resume on page 68.*

Open Netscape by double-clicking on the "Communicator" icon and look in the extreme bottom right-hand corner. See the little envelope going into a tray? Push on it.

We set up your e-mail profile back in chapter 3. If you didn't follow along or you don't remember setting up your mail, go back and take a quick look (pages 31 to 33).

Now that you are all set up, you are now ready to get your e-mail. Point at the little envelope in the top left corner of the screen. When you leave the cursor on it for a second or two, it will pop up a descrip-tion bar. This one says "Get New Mail." Click on the button.

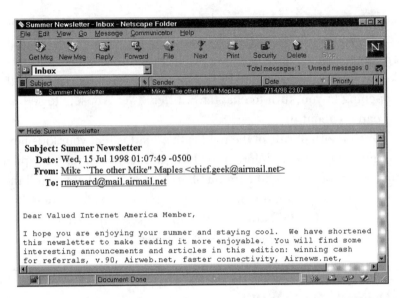

And off Netscape goes to find your e-mail. Now that it's all set up, checking your mail anytime is easy. If you're browsing the Web like we were when we went to Search.com and you want to get your e-mail, just click on the little envelope that's always in the bottom right corner. Netscape will go off automatically and get it for you.

The e-mail section of Netscape (called a Window by most people) is simple to use. In the top left-hand square are your various mail-boxes. Most people use just the three that Netscape starts with. The "Inbox" is where new e-mail arrives. "Sent" is where you keep a copy of everything you or your kids sent to anyone. Already I can tell you see the value of that little folder . . . parents are sneaky too, right? The "Trash" section holds all the mail that you or your kids have tried to erase. Another very useful section for parents.

The main window is where the messages in each mailbox are listed. In this example, the messages in my Inbox are listed by the date and time they were sent. You can tell new messages because they will appear in **bold** print. To read any message, just click once and the message appears in the long gray window on the bottom of the screen.

To respond to any message, click on the little envelope on the toolbar that says "Reply." It will always give you a choice of replying only to the author, or, if there were multiple recipients of the original message, you can send your reply to all of them automatically.

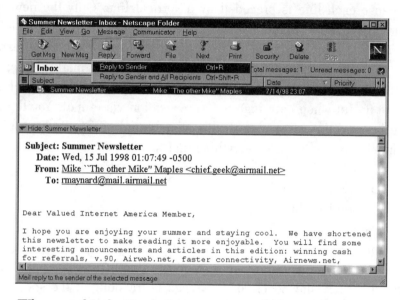

When you hit the Reply button, a new window appears on top of the others. You will notice that the address and subject fields are already filled in.

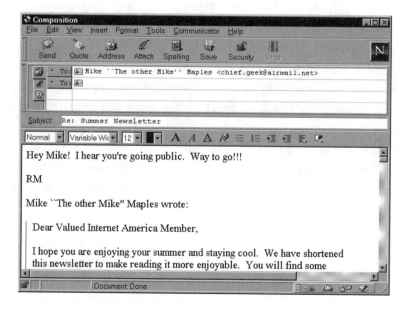

In this case, I'm responding to the welcome message that comes in every copy of Netscape Messenger. You can tell what they said because each line is preceded by a vertical line. Only the newest e-mail programs use these vertical lines. Older programs use the left carat ">." What I wrote is on the top and appears to be normal text.

Putting quotes from previous conversations and marking them, either with a vertical line or a left carat, is called "threading" and is quite useful when carrying on a conversation via e-mail. You'll get the hang of threading almost immediately and once you do, you'll wonder why we don't do everything that way:

>>>> I started this whole conversation like this.

>>> Then you said this.

>>Then I said that.

>Then you said this.

And now I'm responding to you with this.

Once you are done with your response, simply press the button to "Send" and poof! your message is traveling at the speed of l i g h t and will be waiting the next time the recipient checks his mail.

To send a new message to someone, just push the second button from the left marked "New Message." It's supposed to resemble a pen on a piece of paper.

Simply address the new message to whoever you want, being extremely careful to type in the e-mail exactly, watching for both punctuation and CaSe. Type in a subject in the subject line, and then type your message. Click on Send when you're ready, and off it goes.

Once you are done with your e-mail, simply close the e-mail portion of Netscape by clicking on the "x" in the upper right-hand corner, or the little wheel in the bottom right corner. You should return to the web-browsing window immediately.

Sending and receiving e-mail using Explorers 🅔 only. Navigators 🖳 go to page 75.

Look in the bottom left corner of the taskbar (that's the gray bar that stays up when all your programs are running). The extreme left corner should have the ▦Start button. Look just to the right of it. You will see this little toolbar: 🅔 🖳 📝 🖉

This is called the Active Desktop Toolbar. It's quite handy and lets you start programs that you use frequently by clicking once on the icon for the program that you want. In this instance, we want the button with the little "e" and the envelope. This will start "Outlook Express," one of the simplest and most powerful e-mail programs around. Certainly, it has the right price . . . it's FREE!

Click on the "Outlook Express" icon. The first time you do this, you will probably get a message asking you if you want to use Outlook Express as your default e-mail client.

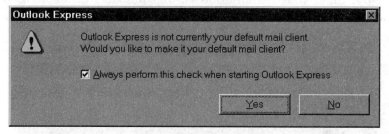

If you are not using AOL or Netscape for mail, select "Yes." You will then see the next screen asking you to set up the program. Don't worry, you only have to do this once and it's very easy.

You may or may not be asked whether you want to set up a new Internet Mail Account. If you do, then click on the button that says "Set up a new Internet Mail Account" and click "Next." Otherwise, with Outlook Express open, select "Tools," then "Accounts," and click on the "Mail" tab and "Add." Either way, you will then see this screen:

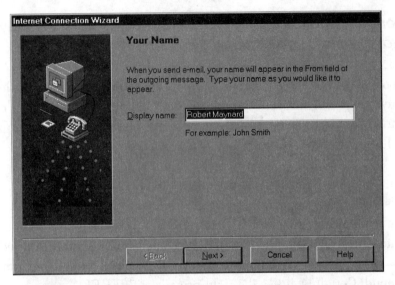

Enter your name, or, if one of your kids will be using this account, their name. See, I told you this was easy. When you're done, click "Next."

Now, input your e-mail address. You probably got it from your Internet Provider. If you're not sure, give them a call and they'll help you.

Now the software needs to know the names of the computers that will be holding and sending your e-mail. Your electronic post offices, if you will. Be sure that you input the computers that are correct for your ISP. Unless you are an Internet America customer, the computers listed in this example will be useless to you. The POP mail computer for Mindspring is mail.mindspring.com. The SMTP mail server is mail.mindspring.com. If you use another ISP you will need to contact their support group for the names.

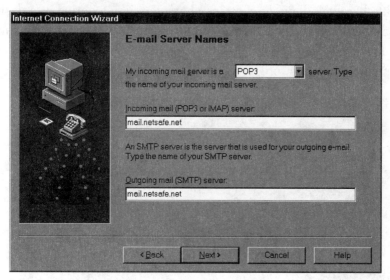

"SMTP" and "POP3" are two of the "Protocols" I mentioned earlier. You remember, the Geeks use fancy acronyms so they make us believe that there is some magic in what they do. In this case, the letters are pretty straightforward. SMTP is the Simple Mail Transport Protocol and POP3 is the Post Office Protocol, revision 3. Of course, you don't really need to know any of this, except to impress your kids and perhaps troubleshoot a problem if you have trouble sending or receiving e-mail.

The thing that you need to worry about is that you input the name of the server(s) precisely as your ISP has given them to you. Remember, everything here is CaSe SenSITiVe. So, enter the name of your ISP's SMTP server here. Then click "Next."

Make sure that you've selected POP3 as the Mail Server Type.

IMAP is a new mail standard that will become more prominent in 1999 and later. For now, an IMAP server is extremely rare and you will know if you have one.

Once you have filled in the correct information and you are certain there are no typos, click the "Next" button.

You will now be asked for your e-mail username and password. Your username is usually the letter combination in front of the @ sign in your e-mail address. However, if your e-mail address is more than eight characters long, or contains characters like a period or a dash, it will be different, as is the case in my username. If you are not sure of your username, check with the support group of your ISP. When you enter your password, remember that it is CaSE SensITive.

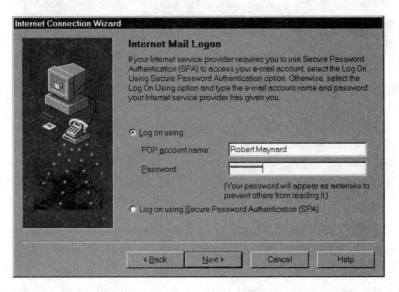

The program would now like you to assign a name to this account that you will recognize. It defaults to the mail-server name, which isn't too friendly, if you ask me. Select a name that you like. Keep in mind that everyone in the family can use Outlook Express and have their e-mail stay private, so you'll want to be able to identify the mail account easily.

Finally, Outlook Express wants to know how you will be connecting to the Internet. In nearly all cases, you will be using a modem. Click the appropriate box as I have below.

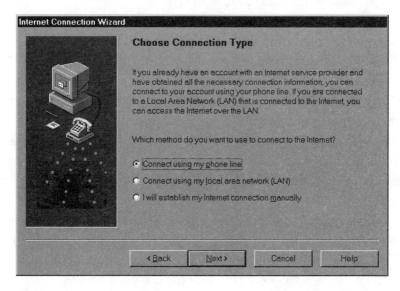

You are now ready to get your e-mail. Outlook Express automatically goes out to the Internet to check for any mail you have and returns it to you on this screen.

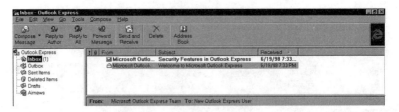

The top row is called the toolbar. Each of the buttons is self-explanatory. "Reply to All" simply sends a message to anyone who was a recipient of the original message you have in front of you.

The top window lists all the messages you have, unread messages will appear in **bold** typeface and the little envelope will be closed.

To reply to any message, simply click on the "Reply to Author button." A new window will appear with the original message quoted. Type what you want to say and then click on the little whizzing envelope to send it on its way. It's that easy.

To send a new message, simply click on the New Message icon, type your message, click the whizzer and your message is traveling at light speed.

Once you are done with your e-mail, close the program by clicking on the "x" in the upper right-hand corner.

As you can see, once you get it set up, e-mail is incredibly easy. As you start using it, you'll wonder how you ever got along without it. My dad has become an e-mail addict, regularly sending me jokes, notes, and encouragement through this great communications medium.

As e-mail becomes more pervasive in your home, you may want to think about getting separate addresses for each of the family members who use it. Contact your ISP when the time comes for this next step.

One more little trick to help you keep an eye on your kids. Directly under the toolbar, you will find the Folders list. See that list of mailboxes? These will be very useful for you to keep an eye on your kids' correspondence. Let me show you what I mean.

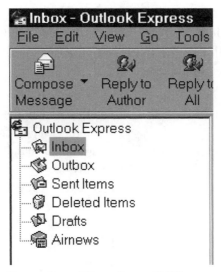

From the list, select "Sent Items." When you do, violà! Every-thing that has been sent from your computer is listed. This can lead to some very interesting reading, to say the least.

Check the Sent Items box every few weeks, or whenever you feel so inclined. What you read there will likely give you plenty of fodder for your next dinner-table conversation.

Both Navigators 🌀 and Explorers 🅔

You and your kids will quickly find that it is sometimes difficult in e-mail communication to get across what you really mean because you can't send inflections, tones of voice, or even emphasis like **bold** or <u>underlined</u> words. So, the Internet community has developed a few tricks to make it easier. If you want to shout, simply type in ALL CAP-ITAL LETTERS. To smile when you say something, type ":->" without the quotation marks. (Turn your head ninety degrees to the left and you'll see what I mean.) Then there are a handful of acronyms that we use to shorten what we have to type. For instance: TIA means "Thanks In Advance." This shorthand for emotions is called an "emoticon."

For instance, if I want to poke fun at someone and I were in person, I might give them a wink and a smile ;^> or if I were particularly per-turbed, I might YELL AT THEM THE ENTIRE TIME. If someone told me an especially good joke, I'd probably LOL (laugh out loud). The possibilities are endless. Here are some of the most common emoticons and acronyms. You'll have fun trying to figure them out.

ADN Any Day Now

AFK Away From Keyboard

B4N Bye for Now

BBS Bulletin Board Service

BIF Basis In Fact

BL Belly Laughing

BRB Be Right Back

BTW By The Way

CU See you

CUL8R See you Later

DTRT Do The Right Thing

FAQ Frequently Asked Question

FISH First In, Still Here

FYI For Your Information

GAL Get A Life

GIWIST Gee, I Wish I Said That

IAC In Any Case

IC I See

ILY I Love You

IME In My Experience

IMHO In My Humble Opinion

IOW In Other Words

L8R Later

LOL Laughing Out Loud

NBIF No Basis In Fact

OIC Oh, I See

POV Point Of View

ROFL Rolling On Floor Laughing

ROFLAHMS Rolling On Floor
    Laughing And Holding My
    Sides

TTBOMK To The Best Of My
    Knowledge

WFM Works For Me

: -) Smiley with Nose

:) Smiley without nose

:-> Another Happy Face

:*) Clowning Around

%-} Silly

:-r Bleahh (sticking tongue out)

:-f Smirk

:-| Disgusted

:-! Foot in Mouth

:-J Tongue in cheek comment

:-o Shouting

:-b Tongue stuck out

: - (Frown

:-x Kiss

[[name]] hug!

:-X Not saying a word

Î-) Wink

(-_-) Secret Smile

:@ What???

How do you find someone's e-mail address so you can send a message? The easiest way to do this is to simply call them up and ask them. But you can also try one of the more interesting sites on the Internet which catalogs everyone's e-mail address and allows you to search for someone based on their real name and general location on the Internet. It's called WhoWhere.com.

Using your browser, type in www.WhoWhere.com in the address line. And you arrive at the WhoWhere home page.

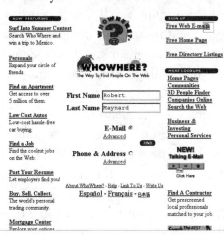

Say you wanted to search for me, Robert Maynard, to send me an e-mail and tell me how great you think this book is so far. Simply type in my name and click the Search WhoWhere button. The computers at WhoWhere search their files, which they have gathered by trolling the Internet for published e-mail addresses. You can see from the answers we got, that although the first two are not me, the next three e-mail addresses are and you can get mail to me at any of them.

The advanced features of WhoWhere can also help you find mailing addresses and some personal information about people (address, telephone number, employer, social security number, credit history, etc.) although this function is still rather unpredictable. In the coming years, WhoWhere will probably become the definitive

site on the Internet to locate people. Woe to those people who don't pay their child support. Skip tracing just became a whole lot easier.

E-mail will draw your kids to the computer like nothing else. You won't have to encourage them to go online if they think there is any possibility that they might have some mail waiting for them. Ask your ISP about separate e-mail boxes for your kids. The two that we recommend offer separate family mailboxes for a nominal monthly fee.

If you have e-mail at your office, send some to the kids once in awhile. If you can get into the habit of this, you'll find that they will talk to you with their computers about things that would never have occurred to them otherwise. You will also encourage them to learn to put their thoughts and emotions into writing, setting them apart from their peers in most cases.

Several sites around the Internet act as clearing houses for kids to get e-pals. An e-pal is just like a pen pal, only they use e-mail to communicate. Check the Kids Links section of our Web page at www.goodparents.com to find easy directions to the best e-pal lists in the world.

Internet e-mail is great. Once you or your kids start using it, you will find that your writing skills improve quickly, and your kid's view of the world will expand dramatically.

Chapter Six

Usenet News

W ELCOME TO THE WILD WEST. Although the Geeks call it "News," it's anything but. The Usenet is a vast array of discussion groups, called "newsgroups," where anything goes. And when I say "anything," I mean *anything*.

A newsgroup is an area on the Internet devoted to the discussion of a specific topic. The groups are usually named for their topic. For instance, you would presume that the newsgroup named alt.fan.amy.grant was a place where fans of singer Amy Grant go to talk to each other. You would be exactly right.

At last count, there were something like twenty-nine thousand newsgroups, dedicated to every subject you can imagine, and many that you can't. I find newsgroups fascinating because you can meet and talk with people from literally every corner of the world who share your interests. You can also listen in on the conversations of some of the greatest minds in the world. Imagine if you could have watched an argument between Ernest Hemingway and F. Scott Fitzgerald on literary style, or between Albert Einstein and J. Robert Oppenheimer on the nature of the atom. Those arguments and discussions are out there now between the next generation of Einsteins and Oppenheimers. The possibilities are endless when you think about it.

However, the Usenet is also where much of the pornography, software piracy, and criminal activity occurs. I strongly recommend that children under fourteen be restricted from News. There are some redeeming qualities to the Usenet, but the risks in this completely uncontrolled environment far outweigh any benefit younger children might gain from accessing this feature. If you have installed CYBER-sitter, enforcing a ban on Usenet is simple. If you use NetShield, News is not even acessible. I know of no other way to completely block News from your computer when your kids are using it.

The Usenet is the ultimate cooperative endeavor. All over the world, Geeks have built computers called News Servers. These computers are constantly talking to other News Servers around the Internet. They are checking to see if they all have the same information all the time. When something new appears on one server, it sends it off to all the others so they can update themselves. As this happens, everyone on the Internet can see it.

As far as anyone knows, there are about five million people working on as many as one hundred thousand different news servers, producing over six gigabytes of information (the equivalent of about six hundred books the size of Webster's dictionary) every day. That number is growing at the rate of about 100 percent per year. Unfortunately, most of this data volume is pornographic or adult-oriented material.

The Usenet is broken down into areas called "hierarchies." These are further broken down into newsgroups like the one I described earlier for Amy Grant. There are nine major hierarchies, which house most of the more than twenty-four thousand newsgroups on the Internet. They are:

alt: By far the hierarchy with the most groups. The alt groups run the gamut from harmless, highly targeted discussions like alt.fan.amy.grant to the most disgusting pictures you can imagine like alt.binaries.pictures.erotica.children to groups dedicated to software piracy to computer hacker groups dedicated to what they consider the fine art of unauthorized access to computer networks. Anyone can form an alt group and the alt groups are far and away the most popular area of Usenet, primarily because they house most of the pornography.

Comp: These groups are dedicated primarily to the discussion of computer-oriented issues like hardware and programming.

Rec: Dedicated to the discussion of recreational activities (hiking, fishing, etc.).

Soc: Primarily dedicated to the discussion of social topics like alcoholism, disease, support groups, and the like.

Sci: For the discussion of scientific issues. This is where you will find some of the most gifted minds in the world talking about the latest in science. This is a great tool for research.

News: This hierarchy deals with the administration of Usenet and is virtually unintelligible to all but the most die-hard Geeks.

Talk: Primarily used to argue about things like politics and to kibbutz on virtually anything you can imagine.

Misc: You guessed it, for miscellaneous issues which don't fall in any of the above.

There are hundreds of other hierarchies, but these are the big ones.

Undoubtedly, your ISP will have a hierarchy to discuss issues pertinent to them. You will usually find that they start with the domain name that you use for your e-mail, for instance, Netcom customers find their newsgroups are named netcom.general, among others. Your ISP's newsgroups are an important place to stay informed on what's going on and to meet people in your area who are on the Internet. Mindspring customers will find their internal newsgroups in mindspring.general.

So, now that you are completely confused, let's take a look at news.

Navigators 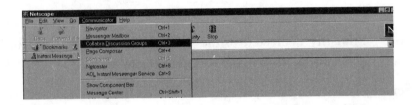 Only. Explorers 𝒆 go to page 86.

Double-click on the Navigator icon ![icon], and we'll get going. Netscape will start by showing the home page you have set as its default. This would be Yahooligans if you've taken my advice. From there, select Communicator and Collabra Discussion Groups. (If you don't see a selection for Communicator, you have an older version of the software. Select Window and then News instead.)

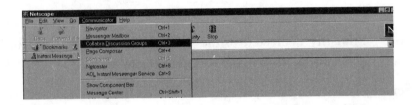

You will see the main News window for Netscape. I'm not going to teach you how to actually use news. Instead, I'm going to teach you how to find out if your kids are using it and what they are doing with it. If you want to figure out how to use Netscape News, go to http://www.udel.edu/evelyn/netnews.html for a great step-by-step tutorial.

Netscape's new discussion group software, called Collabra, which I show here, has a radically different look and feel from its older versions. However, the concepts are the same, and you should be able to work your way through it even if you have an older version.

Newsgroups also have pictures. In fact, that's where some of the most disgusting pornography you can imagine is located and viewing it is ridiculously easy. Allow me to show you. Make sure you are in the news window of Netscape, either by selecting Window and News, or Communicator and Collabra. If using Collabra, select the subscribe button.

You will come to a screen containing a list of all the available newsgroups out there on your ISP's news servers. If you don't see anything, or if the program asks if you want to get a list of newsgroups, that's good news (no pun intended). It means no one in your home is using Netscape to get to the Usenet.

But the more likely scenario, especially if you have a teenage son, is that the newsgroups have been accessed at least once. Click the tab that says Search for a newsgroup, type: alt.binaries.pictures.erotica in the dialog box and click Okay. Netscape will now go out to the Internet and pull all the newsgroups in this subset.

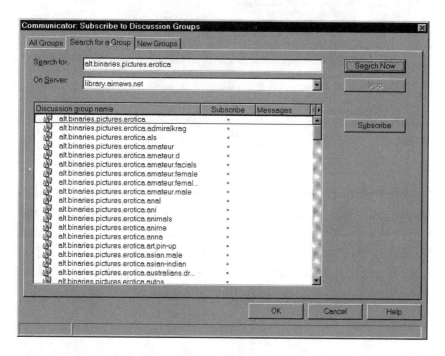

Here you see that there are more than five hundred different newsgroups that start with alt.binaries.pictures.erotica. They are all pornographic and they range the gamut of every conceivable sexual pecadillo. So, select one of the groups (I just selected the first one on the list), and here come 14,890 different pornographic images. No charge, no appropriateness or age checks, nothing of the sort.

Perhaps now you see why we block Usenet entirely at NetSafe and through CYBERsitter. I apologize for the graphic nature of the following material, but there is really no delicate way to do this. In the parts that seem just gratuitously graphic, we've blacked out the really offensive words and pictures.

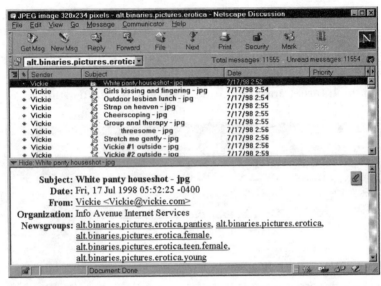

Most pictures in these groups are stored in a special kind of format call .jpg (pronounced "J-PEG"). In this instance, you will notice that the first article in the list is called "White Panty House Shot.jpg" The ".jpg" extension is a clear indicator that this is a picture. So, we click on it and, lo and behold, it's a picture, one of the more benign pictures on the Net, in fact.

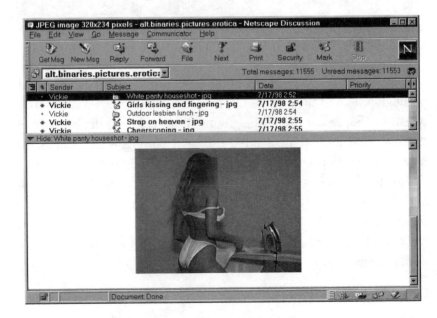

I spent several years in the service and saw my share of pornography. But, I must say, that I have been shocked by some of the stuff I've seen in the newsgroups. (Research, honey, I swear!) This whole process took about fifteen seconds and the computers couldn't care less if you're twelve or fifty.

Netscape is probably the only Usenet newsreader that does not save News postings to the hard drive before displaying them. No doubt, however, your son or daughter, if he or she gets into this, will end up saving one or two favorites. As they get more involved in Usenet, they will probably move on to a more sophisticated newsreader. All of the hard-core news programs save the images on your local hard disk.

Here's how you find out if your kids are looking at this kind of adult material. Usually, when you want to look at a picture on Usenet, it must first be downloaded to your computer as a file before it can be displayed. Each file will be saved as a JPEG. That means you only have to check your computer for files ending in ".jpg" to see if they've been looking at the stuff.

To find a file on your computer, point your mouse at the <Insert Start button.tif> in the bottom left-hand corner and click one time. You will see a short menu pop up from the bottom. Select "Find" as I've indicated here, roll the mouse to the right, and click on "Files or Folders."

In the dialog box that pops up, enter "*.jpg" without the quotation marks. An asterisk (*) is called a "wild card" by the Geeks, but you and I can just call it a "splat." We have asked

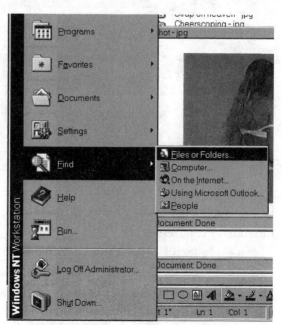

the computer to find all JPEG pictures that may be on our computer. Press the "Find Now" button.

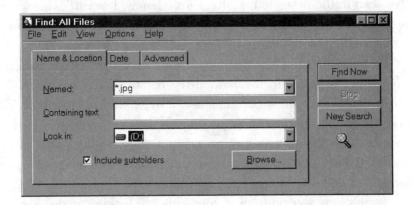

And, woe unto the kid who gets caught, there she is . . .

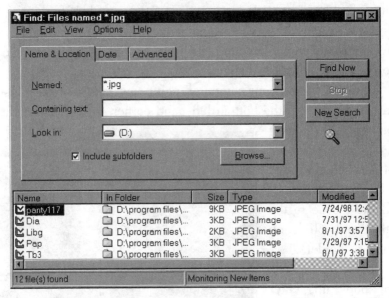

To view the picture, just double-click on the file that you think looks suspicious, and in a few seconds you should have ample fuel for your next parent-kid talk.

One reader of a preliminary version of this volume sent me a letter of thanks for this little tidbit of information. Seems her fifteen-year-old son was telling her that he was always doing his homework until late in the night. She went into his computer and ran a .jpg search and found more than one thousand pictures, none of which he would have wanted his mom to know about. Needless to say, she had something to say about it.

Explorers 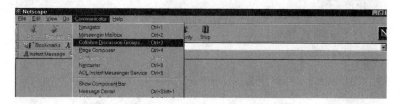 only. Navigators resume on page 95.

Double-click on the Explorer icon and we'll get started. Explorer should open and, once your modem connects, it will show you the home page you have set as its default. If you've taken my advice, that will be Yahooligans. From there, select "Mail," and then "Read News."

The first time you do this, Explorer will launch a wizard that walks you through the setup process. If you don't see this prompt, skip to page 90 while the rest of us walk through the setup process.

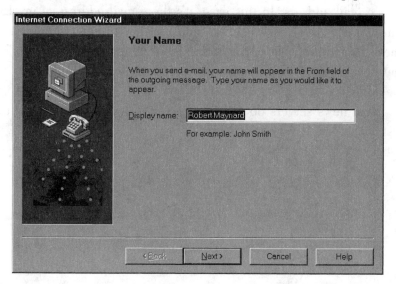

Click on the "Next" button to proceed. The first question asks for your name and e-mail address. Be careful that you don't make any mistakes here.

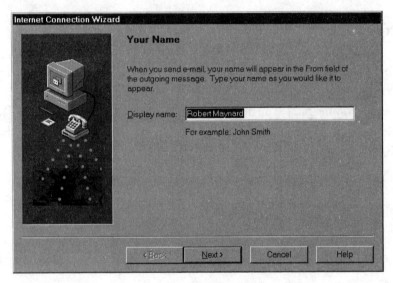

Next, Microsoft News wants to know the name of the computer (News Server) you will be using to access Usenet News. This is usually the word "news" followed by a dot (.) and then the last part of your e-mail address. In this case, it's the e-mail address of my ISP "airmail.net". The news-server address for Internet America is "news.airmail.net." For Mindspring it is "news.mindspring.com." If you have another ISP, check with their technical support group for the address.

Most news servers do not require you to log in so disregard the rest of the panel and click "Next."

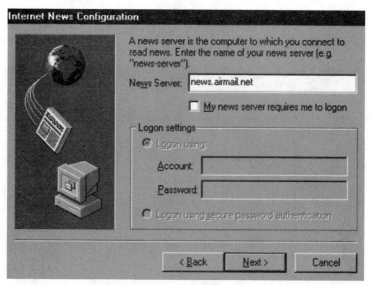

Now Microsoft News wants to know how you will be connecting to the Internet. In nearly all cases, you will be connecting with a modem. Click the appropriate button. Make sure you push the drop-down arrow and highlight the name of the connection you will be using. In most cases, you will have only one choice. Click "Next."

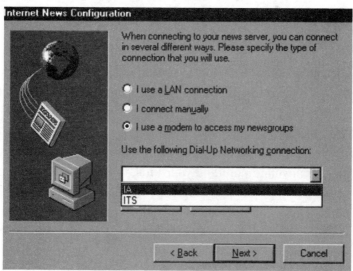

The setup Wizard now tells you that you are done and how to change information should you ever need to. Click on "Finish."

Next, the program wants to go out and find all the different newsgroups on your ISP's news server. This will likely take awhile since there are so many.

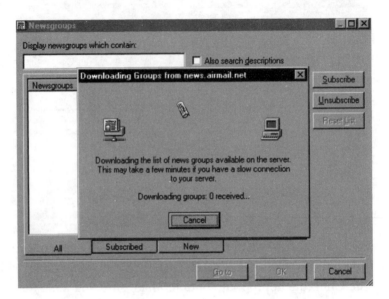

Once the news server dumps all the newsgroups into your software, you will see a long list of cryptic newsgroup headings. I'm not going to teach you how to actually use and participate in Usenet news. My goal here is to give you enough information to find out if your kids are into News and, if they are, to find out what they are doing. If you want to learn how to use Microsoft News for yourself, go to http://www.microsoft.com/ie/most/howto/mailnews.htm for a primer on getting the most out of Microsoft News.

While many newsgroups have written discussions, the most active groups have explicit pictures and adult text. This is how incredibly easy it is for anyone, including your kids, to find this material. In the space title "Display Newsgroups which contain" type "erotica" as I have here. "Erotica" is the euphemism that Geeks use for pornography. The software will diligently search for the beginning of the erotica newsgroups and list them alphabetically for you. As you can see if you scroll down the list, there are more than four hundred of these groups, dedicated to any kind of pornography you can imagine, and some that you probably can't, like alt.binaries.pictures.erotica.bestiality.hamsters.duct-tape (I don't even want to know about this one).

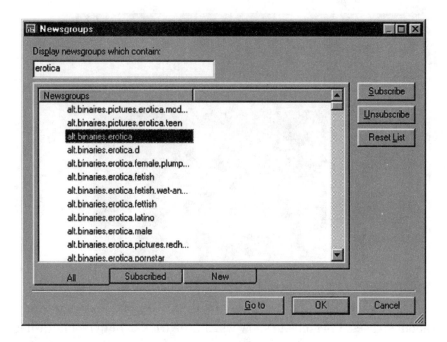

You will notice that the two newsgroups directly above the one we are looking for are dedicated to child pornography. Now you know why I strongly recommend blocking News with CYBERSitter or Net-Shield.

All your children need to do to view any of this is to simply select alt.binaries.pictures.erotica by pointing on it and clicking the left mouse button one time. Then by selecting the "Go To" button on the bottom of the page, they will soon get a list of all the "articles" available at the time. (You need to know what your children could be accessing.)

You can easily tell a picture, since the title will usually include the ".jpg" extension. This is a form of compression that computers use to make pictures smaller to store. To view it, simply double-click on the article. It might take a minute or two to download, but very quickly, the software efficiently presents you with your prize.

The top portion of the window is reserved for any text comments. The little [paperclip icon] in the bottom window tells you that there is a picture included. To view it, simply double-click on the article name.

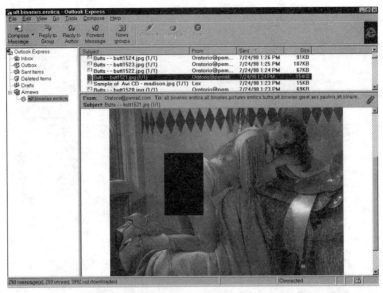

Sometimes, the first time you do this, the software posts a warning about viruses. I'm going to show you a little trick to help monitor what the kids are doing. Leave the button clicked on for "Save It to Disk," then click on the box that asks "Always ask before opening this type of file." That should turn the checkmark off. I'll show you how to use this to monitor your kids' activities in a few minutes.

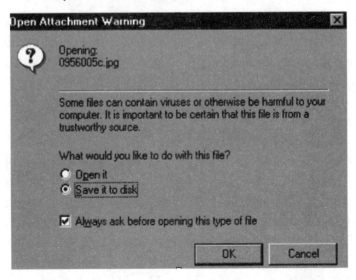

According to my newsreader, there were some thirty-nine thousand pornographic pictures and messages in this one newsgroup alone. The amount and explicit nature of sexual material available on Usenet is truly mind-boggling. When I was in the service, I saw my share of pornography, but what is freely available on the Internet through these newsgroups could shock the most tolerant among us.

Remember when I told you to save the file and turn off the warning? Now every time you or your kids view a picture like this in News, it will be saved to your hard disk, leaving a trail a mile wide for you to find.

Here's how you find out if your kids are looking at forbidden material. Usually, when you want to look at a picture on Usenet, it must first be downloaded to your computer as a file before it can be displayed. Each file will be saved as a JPEG. That means you only have to check your computer for files ending in ".jpg" to see what they've been viewing.

To find a file on your computer, point your mouse at the "Start" button in the bottom left-hand corner and click one time. You will see a short menu pop up from the bottom. Select "Find" as I've indicated here, then roll the mouse to the right and click on "Files or Folders."

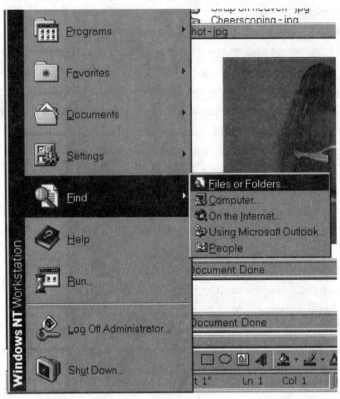

In the dialog box that pops up, enter "*.jpg" without the quotation marks. An asterisk "*" is called a wild card by the Geeks, but you and I can just call it a "splat." We have asked the computer to find all JPEG pictures that may be on our computer. Press the "Find Now" button.

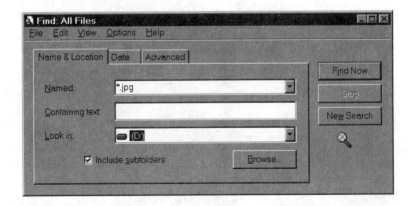

And, woe unto the kid who gets caught, there she is...

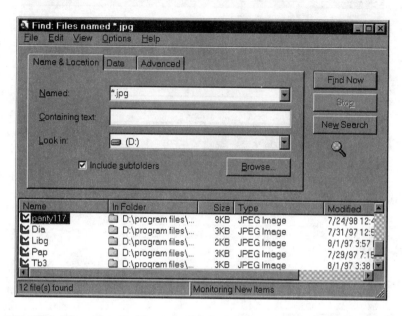

To view the picture, just double-click on the file that you think looks suspicious, and in a few seconds you should have ample fuel for your next parent-kid talk.

Both Navigators and Explorers

Your kids can join in on virtually any discussion anywhere on the Internet and you'll never be able to tell what they're doing from the Netscape or Explorer newsreader. However, there's a great secret weapon for parents. It's called Dejanews and it keeps track of everything just about anyone has ever done on the Usenet.

Close the News window by clicking on the "x" in the top right-hand corner. You should now be back at the Yahooligans Web site with either browser. In the address block, type in: www.dejanews.com and hit the return key.

Click on the "Power Search" icon and then on "Create A Query Filter" and we'll see what your kids are talking about.

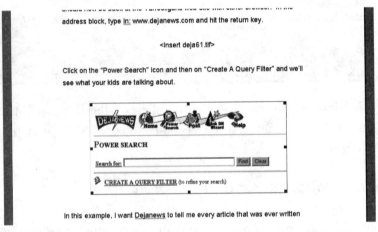

In this example, I want Dejanews to tell me every article that was ever written from one of my e-mail addresses. Your kid's e-mail address is the best thing to search for because it is completely unique on the Internet. Notice that in many of the spaces, I have entered a splat (*). That tells the Dejanews computers to search for everything.

QUERY FILTER

Fill in any or all of the fields below to limit what records will be searched when you

▶ Show expanded Query Filter form with examples - New!

Newsgroup(s): |* |

Browse Usenet Newsgroups! - New!

Freeform date(s)*: |* |

From*: | | To*: | |

*Use Freeform date(s) or From/To.

Author(s): |rmaynard@airmail.net |

Subject(s): |* |

[Create Filter] [Clear Filter]

Once you have filled in the e-mail address and the splats like I've shown you, push the "Create Filter" button and in just a few seconds Dejanews will retrieve every article your children have ever written on the Internet's Usenet systems. In this case, three articles are found.

articles are found.

FILTERED POWER SEARCH

Search for: | | [Find] [Clear]

This search will be on the filtered set below.

💲 **QUERY FILTER (RESULTS)**

Filter size:	**3 documents**		
Newsgroup(s):	All		
Date(s):	All	Change	Clear
Author(s):	rmaynard@airmail.net	Filter	Filter
Subject(s):	All		

Click on the hyperlink that shows the number of documents to start reviewing them and, as importantly, the groups to which they are posted.

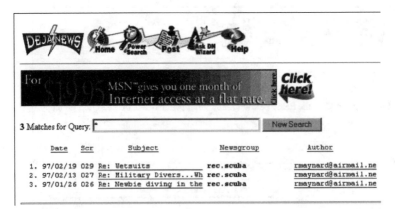

To read any of the articles, simply click on the hyperlinks of the title in the third column. In this case I clicked on the third one, "Newbie Diving . . . ." As you can see, Usenet follows the same convention as e-mail, in threaded discussions. Here, someone is asking advice on where to take an inexperienced diver on their first dives.

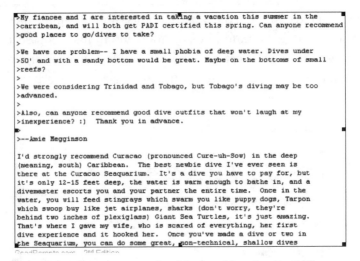

The original question is highlighted by the ">." You can tell my response since there is nothing in front of it. The fourth column on the search list shows the newsgroups that they appear in. You'll be able to tell very quickly if your kids are into something they shouldn't be. Watch for really cryptic newsgroup titles, especially in the alt hierarchy. For instance, alt.2600 is for a revolutionary group of young hackers around the world.

After you read a few of your kids' postings, it's time for another one of those great dinner-table conversations.

"Interesting post you made about diving in Curaçao. I didn't know you could dive," you say with a twinkle in your eye as you watch the blood drain from your child's face.

This time she is so shocked that you have rendered her simply speechless.

Usenet News can be productive, fun, and informative but, in my opinion, it is the most dangerous place on the Internet for kids to hang out. News is also the best reason to keep the computer in a public area and to install CYBERSitter or get Internet access from NetShield. The CYBERSitter child-protection software will allow you to prevent your children from accessing the Usenet at all without your permission each time they try. NetShield, on the other hand, simply does not allow the news protocol through their systems, period. If you're not going to use NetShield, I strongly recommend using CYBERsitter to block access to Usenet if your youngsters are under age fourteen, or show any propensity toward mischief in this area. For detailed instructions on blocking News with CYBERsitter, see chapter 10.

——————————————■——————————————

Chapter Seven

Chat

A H, THE JOYS OF PARENTING. There you are, reading your paper after dinner and your teenage son walks up to you unbidden and says, "Dad, I want to chat."

"Okay, son, have a seat. Let's chat."

Your son looks at you like you just grew a third eye while asking him to eat brussel sprouts. "Not with you. I want to chat on the computer. Can you show me how?"

"Oh, of course. What could I have been thinking? Sure I can show you. Come on."

Internet Chat can best be described as real-time e-mail, or Newsgroup postings. In essence, you sit at your computer at the same time that I sit at mine and we type back and forth to each other in real time. Others can join in like an old-fashioned party line and we can discuss anything imaginable. There really isn't much to chat, but kids dominate the medium and they almost universally love it.

There are not many ways to get into trouble if you make sure the kids follow this simple rule:

Tell them to never give out their real name, address, phone

number, or school name. If you follow my advice and install CYBER-
sitter as described in chapter 10, they will have to get your permission to transmit this data anyway.

They should treat every person they meet in chat as a stranger,
and until they've had a chance to introduce them to you over the net,
they should just use their first name or a nickname, called a "handle"
by those who chat.

Finally, tell them that they should never enter a "private room"
with another person. The bulk of all chat-related problems occur
when an adult, posing as a child, lures a kid into a private session.
For some reason these sickos, called "Bears" in Internet parlance,
find it erotic to get kids into sexually explicit discussions in chat.

There is a Protocol on the Internet called Internet Relay Chat
(IRC). It is something of an older legacy system on the Net and is
completely anarchic, much like Usenet. If you have kids under age
fourteen, I recommend that you block access to this type of chat
through CYBERsitter. It's the only software I know of that can keep
your kids out of the IRC system altogether. Details on using CYBER-
sitter to block IRC are available in chapter 10. NetShield also does
not allow IRC through its systems at all, so if you use NetShield as
your ISP, you don't have to worry about this issue at all.

The Web has much better and more controlled chat areas now
that will give your kids what they are looking for, while giving you
peace of mind. Time for another one of those displays of your Internet
prowess. "Okay, son. Go ahead and connect to the Internet and open

Netscape or Explorer. Now,
let's go to www.wbs.net.
They have the best chat
servers on the Internet."
Bookmark this (or add it to
your "Favorites" list in Explorer) the first time you go
so the kids can get back
there easily the next time.

The Webchat Broad-
casting System provides a

relatively secure, monitored environment for kids and adults to chat on the Internet. One of the most important components for control of the environment is to know who everyone is. Before you or your kids can participate in chat, WBS insists that you register and have a valid e-mail address. You need only register one time. After that, the kids will be able to go straight into chat anytime.

Registration is simple and free. Click on "New Users" at the top of the screen. Then follow the links to "Register."

Your child's handle is the way he will be known and addressed in the chat world. WBS has over one million registered users, so most of the intuitive names have already been taken. Try adding some numbers after your selection to help increase the chances that the handle is approved. The form is very simple to fill out and only takes a minute or so.

WBS will send a confirming e-mail to the address you gave them in your registration form. It should only take a few minutes to arrive and you need to send it back to them so that they activate your account. Check your

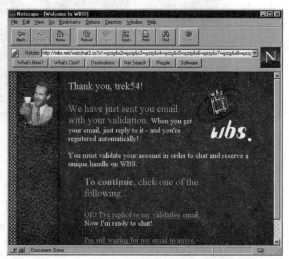

mail using the explanation I outlined in chapter 4. Once the mail arrives from WBS, simply send it back and you'll be ready to go.

After you have responded to the e-mail, it's time to begin chatting. Close the e-mail window in Netscape or Explorer by clicking on the little "X" in the top right-hand corner. You should now be back at the WBS sign-up page. Click on "OK, I've responded to my e-mail and I'm ready to chat."

As the parent, your part of the exercise is nearly over. You'll be able to return to your newspaper in just a few minutes, secure in the fact that your child is chatting in an area where there is at least a little bit of structure and system administrators who will help if someone gets too unruly.

Follow the simple instructions provided by WBS. When I checked, the kids' areas were a little hard to find. The best places for children are under the "Community" button.

Select one that you want to go to. The numbers in parenthesis

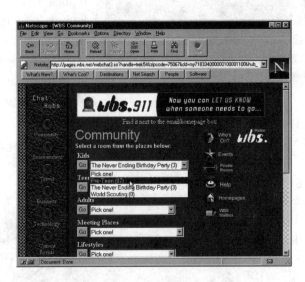

show how many different people are currently in the room (on the party line) talking at that time. We'll go into "Pre-Teen."

Have your child enter his new handle and password in the

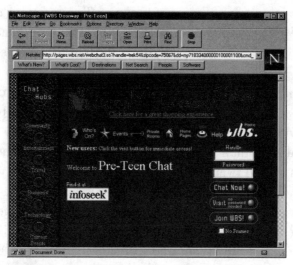

blanks. Remember that the password will be CaSe SensiTiVe, so enter it exactly the way you did the first time. Then press the "Chat Now!" button and you're done!

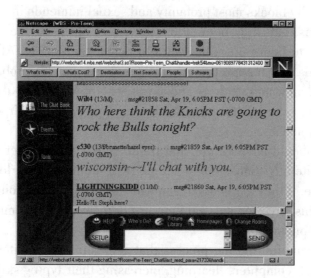

WBS allows your kids to add pictures and sound to their chat experience. Just show them where the "Help" button is on the bottom of the screen and let them go. The other kids in the chat room will be happy to help them learn.

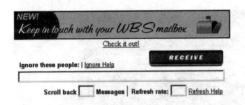

To join into a conversation, just type a message in the box surrounded by the dark field next to the Send button. Your kids can select the color of text and emphasis with the drop-down menus to the left. When they are done, press "Send" and their message will appear in a few seconds.

WBS is staffed twenty-four hours a day, seven days a week with moderators. Tell your kids that if someone is misbehaving in a chat room using profanity or harassing them, they can come get you, or click on the "WBS 911" link in the lower right corner. This will call an adult monitor to the room who will stop the nonsense. WBS can terminate the offender's account.

Just a note about these chat rooms: The first few times I went to the pre-teen room to observe, the favorite topic of conversation with the kids was how to defeat the automatic screening software. WBS automatically blocks most profanity and sexual innuendo in the children's areas, but, kids being kids, they were changing the spelling and trying to figure out other ways to defeat the system. At first, I thought this was inappropriate until I realized that it's probably no different than what they hear and say at school. After a few days, the discussions returned to more innocuous topics, like their favorite music and movies.

WBS should have all the chat traffic your kids will ever want to use with literally thousands of people from around the world online at any time. If they get hooked, you will watch them burn hours upon hours in this environment and then you'll know why I recommended a flat-rate provider.

Chat can often be the process that gets your kids excited about the Internet, computers, learning, increasing their typing skills, and communicating with other kids all over the world. These are great reasons to get them started in chat. Just point them at WBS, remind them to be careful, and it should be a great experience for everyone.

In my opinion, there aren't many reasons why anyone over age sixteen would engage in chat. However, younger kids love it. Now that you've got them started, go back to your paper confident in the fact that they will be spending countless hours talking to people around the world, making new friends, and learning some valuable skills.

Chapter Eight

Net Abuse

YOU AND YOUR KIDS HAVE a right to enjoy the Internet without fear of harassment or offense. Conversely, others on the Internet have the right to enjoy their use of the Internet without being harassed or attacked by anyone operating your computer.

I have the dubious distinction of being an expert in this subject from both sides of the counter. Bad things can happen because of the freedom the Internet provides. You or your kids can be harassed or even stalked by cyber-bullies, or, worse, the FBI might knock on your door one day to tell you that someone has been doing bad things from your computer.

Let me tell you a few true stories from personal experience to give you an idea of just how slippery an issue this can be. I hope you'll learn from them how to safeguard yourself and your family from some of the bad folks out there as well as how to keep your kids from becoming one of the bad guys.

On one side of the issue are those whose sensibilities and values are deeply offended by unconstrained speech. They don't put themselves in situations where they are likely to be exposed to something that offends them in the physical world. But on the Internet, they are often unwittingly exposed to it through no fault of their own.

RULE NUMBER 1: DO NOT ATTEMPT TO HIDE YOUR IDENTITY.

For example, in the summer of 1995, I started receiving numerous complaints that one of my customers was engaging in some very abusive behavior in one of the Usenet news conferences. This newsgroup, alt.fan.amy-grant, was dedicated to the discussion of the Christian singer Amy Grant among those people who admired her. My customer, who attempted to hide his identity to the newsgroup, began posting graphic descriptions of his fantasy of a sexual encounter with Mrs. Grant. The postings were forwarded to me. Even the title "I f——ed Amy Grant" (the author used all the letters) was disgusting to the audience. The text itself would have made Larry Flynt blush.

Now, it's one thing to set up a Web site of your fantasies and invite people to come and see it if they're interested in that sort of thing. It is quite another to post an article in a newsgroup that you know will be abhorrent to the readers. To make matters worse, due to the nature of Usenet, the newsgroup was not able to block the postings. And because the author was attempting to hide his identity, they felt that there was nothing they could do.

This was my first exposure to the issue and I handled it the best way I could. I contacted the customer and asked him to please stop. He said, "Sure, no problem, Robert. Sorry for the heartburn." He then promptly sat down and wrote his next installment. As soon as he finished, he posted it to the newsgroup with a courtesy copy to me. Clearly, he was not going to go away easily.

So, I did the only thing I could. I apologized to the newsgroup personally and on behalf of my company. Then I told them the offender's real name and e-mail address, inviting them to tell him how they felt about his work. Needless to say, with his anonymity stripped, the postings stopped immediately. Okay, maybe it wasn't the only thing I could have done, but it sure seemed to be the right thing to do and it *was* effective. ISPs can cancel an offender's account and work with law enforcement.

The moral of this story is: It's relatively easy to hide your identity from most casual users of the Internet. This anonymity sometimes leads people to engage in behavior that they would normally avoid. Make sure your kids know that deliberately forging someone else's name or hiding their identity in order to cause mischief is a very bad thing. If you find out that they are doing it by using the tactics I gave you earlier, you can take the disciplinary action you think is appropriate. CYBERsitter allows you to ban them from their favorite activities like chat, e-mail, or news. This can be a very effective disciplinary measure, akin to taking the car keys, TV, or phone privileges, and somewhat less drastic than skinning them alive.

RULE #2: IT IS VIRTUALLY IMPOSSIBLE TO STOP SOMEONE FROM PUBLISHING HIS OR HER VIEWS ON THE INTERNET, NO MATTER HOW DISGUSTING THOSE VIEWS MIGHT BE TO MOST OF SOCIETY.

On another side of the issue is the concept of "Freedom of Speech." Our society places a very high value on Patrick Henry's dying declaration: "I may not agree with what you say, but I will defend to the death your right to say it." Indeed, our Constitution's First Amendment holds the right to free speech to be fundamental to a free society. Very good friends of mine have died protecting the Constitution, so I take its content quite seriously.

Later in 1995, I began receiving complaints about a Web site that one of our customers had published using our systems. I went to the site and it was truly disgusting to me. It seemed that this particular customer, who called himself "Bootboy," was a fan of Adolf Hitler and the neo-Nazi Party.

The opening graphic was a picture of two hooded klansmen in the process of splitting open the head of a black man they had captured. It was entitled "The Final Solution." It went on to claim that the Holocaust never happened and was merely a public-relations ploy by Jews to lobby for the state of Israel.

Now, my grandfather was a Jew. He was also an infantryman in Patton's Third Army and one of the first American soldiers to liberate Buchenwald. I remember the look on his face fifty years later when he related the horror of those days. A distant cousin of mine is Elie Weisel, who wrote *Night,* a poignant autobiographical tale of his survival in Auschwitz as a teenager. The point I'm trying to make is that I knew from vivid personal experience that Bootboy was wrong. Not only were his views disgusting, they were outright lies.

The site generated a huge amount of traffic and most of the correspondence I got was in the form of complaints asking me to take the site down and, on the other side, threats of dire physical consequences if I did take the site down. I even received a letter written by a rabbi with the Wiesenthal Center asking me to ban the site. And, as a man of conscience, I wanted to do exactly that.

Unfortunately, I wasn't just a man. I was also the CEO of a company whose customer was using my services within the policies to which we had agreed. (No cracks about conscience and CEO being mutually exclusive.) What he was saying and depicting on his home page was not illegal. It was disgusting, inflammatory, amoral, and totally false, but it was not illegal. To view the site, you had to make a determined effort to go there; it didn't just appear in your e-mail or in a newsgroup where you were forced to look at it. Taking a lesson from Patrick Henry, didn't this man have a right to post his opinion, no matter how radical?

My decision was that he did indeed have that right. I didn't have to like it, but it was not my place to muzzle him. As long as he played by the rules and paid his bills, he had the same rights as everyone else. I had no interest in becoming the arbiter of what would and would not be published on the Internet. Besides, society has a way of taking care of these people. The *Dallas Morning* News ran a front-page Sunday story featuring the site and giving the customer's real name. The Associated Press picked it up and it ran all over the country, and CNN covered it extensively. The man was fired from his job the following day and now lives in Sweden, the last I heard. We took the site down when he violated our Acceptable Use Policies. As far as I know, Bootboy never came back to the Internet.

The moral here is: The Internet is the most powerful vehicle for communication and distribution of ideas in the history of humankind. It has lowered the barriers to entry for people who want to publish their thoughts so that nearly anyone in an industrialized nation with a mind to can publish anything they want to a global audience.

This is a great step forward for intellectual freedom. Unfortunately, this freedom, like all freedom, is a double-edged sword. Certainly China has a lower violent crime rate than the United States, but I don't see many Americans working all their lives to move to that society. Freedom is good, but it comes with responsibility and there will always be those who test its limits.

If you or your child don't want to stumble upon something that is distasteful to you, don't go looking for it. Chances are you will not find anything that you don't want to see. If you do by chance stumble upon a site that gives you the same reaction that I had when looking at Bootboy's, leave quickly and don't go back, just as you wouldn't return to a theater that showed X-rated movies unless you wanted to. If you're using CYBERsitter, you can mark the site so that it will always be blocked. This information will be shared by all the other CYBERsitter users on the Internet, helping them protect their kids as well.

RULE #3: KNOWLEDGE IS POWER. DON'T ABUSE IT.

Then, of course, there are the "practical jokers" who call themselves "hackers" or "crackers." These types were romanticized most effectively by the movie *War Games*. It's natural curiosity for a kid who is good with computers to expand his skills as much and as quickly as possible. For some, that turns to a game of breaking into computers that they find on the Internet. Often this is done just for the thrill of doing it, rather like climbing a mountain because it is there. What you and your kids probably don't know is that this is almost always a federal crime.

In December 1995 (that *was* a very busy year) two FBI agents walked into my office and said, "You, Robert Maynard, are the target of a criminal investigation regarding an attack on a competitor's system that originated from your company's computers." To say I was speechless would be a gross understatement.

It turned out that the investigation was dropped just a few days later because we aggressively assisted the agents in finding out what happened. We did end up disciplining two employees who had decided to play a trick on a competitor. But thankfully, both the company and I were quickly cleared of any suspicion. We ended up training the FBI and other law-enforcement agencies in Internet security and providing expert assistance. But, regardless of the outcome, take it from me, you do not want to find yourself on the wrong end of a badge.

The moral of this story is: If your kids show an inclination to the more technical aspects of the Internet, tell them that before they go into a computer system, they must be invited. Just like in the physical world, even if the door is unlocked, they can still get in a lot of trouble for poking around. If they cause any significant damage—corrupting a company's database or crashing their Web site!—just like in the physical world, odds are that they will eventually find themselves in jail or at least talking to a judge. And you will likely be facing a big bill for the cleanup.

RULE #4: IF A BULLY DECIDES TO PICK ON YOU, LEAVE THE AREA AND NEVER RETURN. YOU WILL NOT BE ABLE TO WIN THE FIGHT.

On yet another side of this issue of appropriate content and use are those who are damaged or terrorized by someone's deliberate acts of aggression in the cyber world. Again, I hope you will learn from my family's personal experience. In late 1996, I was reading one of my regular newsgroups concerning Internet Service Providers in the Dallas/Fort Worth area. I came upon a posting of very graphic and lewd statements about my wife. Of course, the author attempted to hide his identity and went by the name of "Mackdaddy."

Initially, the posts were just despicable taunts attempting to embarrass me, my wife, and my business. For about a week, we just ignored him. Then his posts became more ominous, with thinly veiled threats of violence and attacks on our business and our character. I also started getting e-mail from other victims of this bully.

Eventually, the police informed me that they had discovered the author's true identity and that he was a convicted felon who lived in the area and bragged of violent crimes, robberies, and theft. From the number of e-mails I received from other victims, along with the logs that some of them forwarded to me, it was clear that we had a serious problem. At the urging of the police, I sent my family away to stay with relatives and to ensure their safety.

While this was happening, I was running the largest Internet company in the area. At the time I believed that this was an important newsgroup for me to keep a presence in. All of our employees, many of my customers, the local media, and my competitors read this group regularly. My wife was aghast, I was merely furious. I'm not a very good victim, so I decided to fight back. What a mistake.

When Mackdaddy continued his campaign, even though we politely asked him to stop, I turned to the police. Although they all wanted to help, they had no laws on the books that could put this guy away. They still don't. So, I turned to the civil courts and filed a lawsuit against this bully. We spent more than $60,000 tracking this guy down, getting a Temporary Restraining Order, and going to court. But none of this mattered, since the guy had no respect for the court or the law. As I write this, the case continues. But even if we win, it will be a hollow victory since the defendant is indigent and we will doubtlessly be unable to collect any award. The only thing that will happen is that the legal fees will continue to mount.

A couple of good things came of this, however. We were able to persuade the trial judge that, even though we could not physically locate Mackdaddy or conclusively identify him at the time, we should be able to serve him with our complaint and the Temporary Restraining Order over the Internet. We could confirm that he received the documents with our systems and the help of his Internet provider.

This was a major legal precedent giving other victims like us a significant tool to stop this kind of abuse. Before this ruling, it was usually necessary to physically serve the defendant with a restraining order before it could go into effect, making the bad guy subject to criminal contempt if he violated it. That's fine in the physical world. On the Internet, people are connected at the speed of light. They might be around the corner, or around the world.

In addition, bullies like this never use their real names, so locating them is nearly impossible for most people. The information you need to identify them is in their Internet Provider's records, but they won't release the information without a subpoena. However, you can't get a subpoena without a lawsuit. And you usually can't initiate a lawsuit, without, you guessed it, the bad guy's real name and address. A very frustrating conundrum when it's happening to you.

Ours was a small but significant victory that should make it a bit safer if a sociopath puts you in his sights. Like all perpetrators of abuse, guys like this tend to flee once they are positively identified.

Unfortunately for us, the cost was excessive; not just in money, but peace of mind, personal reputation, and lost productivity in our business while we dealt with the issue. If I had it to do over, I would simply have refused to read or participate in the newsgroup until the abuser lost interest and moved on. If he had continued to pound my e-mail, I would have simply ignored him or changed my address.

The moral of the story is: If a bully like this gets hold of you or your kids, cancel your Internet account immediately, change your e-mail address, and never go back to the place where the bad guy found you. You can fight him like we did, but in my opinion, it's not worth the cost. Even with all the resources we were fortunate to have at our disposal, we were not able to stop him. So, we just started ignoring him. Eventually, he got sick of it and moved on.

If you are in an area of the Internet where kids should be safe and someone begins behaving inappropriately, contact your Internet Provider and ask to speak to their abuse department. This group acts basically like the Internet police and steps in to help when necessary. Indeed, they often work closely with the real police when criminal activity is present. Unfortunately, there isn't much that anyone can do. However, if your ISP seems unconcerned and won't or can't help, immediately cancel your account with that provider and move to another.

That's it on abuse. In short, treat cyberspace the way you treat physical space. Don't say or do anything you don't want your name on. Don't go where you're not invited and don't do anything that you don't want to read about in the Sunday paper. If a bully starts something with you, walk away and never look back. These are good rules for the physical world as well.

Chapter Nine

Using Your GoodParents CD and Our Home Page

NOW IT'S TIME TO INSTALL THE SOFTWARE that I've been talking about throughout the book. In the inside back cover of this book, you should find a CD inside an envelope. If you borrowed this book from a friend and the CD is missing, call us at 800-GoodParents (466–3727) and we'll ship you a new one for a nominal shipping and handling charge. We won't even make you buy the book.

"But, Robert," you say, "I don't have a CD-ROM drive in my computer. I only have a little floppy drive." If you don't have a CD-ROM on your computer, you need to get one. All the educational software on the market today, as well as almost all of the programs being written for your computer, are available only on CD. If your computer is powerful enough to handle it, you can take it to any computer store and ask them to install a CD-ROM for you.

If it's time to get a new computer and you're not sure which one to buy, you can call us at 800-GoodParents and I'll tell you which models I think are the best deals at the time and where to get them. If you have Internet access, please go to our Web site at www.goodparents.com/reviews and get the same information with pictures and links to reviews for the machines that we recommend.

It's not necessary for you to go through every chapter or piece of software that we've included. You can pick and choose those that seem interesting to you and your family.

Chapter 10 provides detailed instructions for installing and using CYBERsitter. Of all the software we've included, I think this is the most important, especially if your kids are under sixteen.

Chapter 11 houses all the software you need to connect to the Internet Providers we recommend in the body of the book. There is literally a wealth of great software here, like Netscape Navigator, Microsoft Explorer, Forte's Agent, games, Internet phone software, and lots of utilities that your kids will love.

This CD and all the software included will work only on computers running Windows 95, Windows NT, or Windows 98. If you haven't bitten the bullet yet and installed Windows 95, now is the time. You can pick up Windows 95 at just about any computer or software store.

Insert the disk in the CD-ROM drive of your computer and close the door, keeping the envelope handy. Our installer shell will automatically start in a few seconds and you will see this:

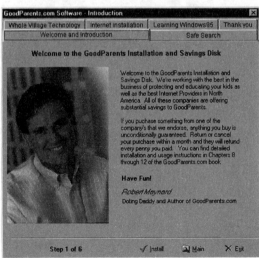

Yes, that's me. At this point, you can either elect to take a guided tour through each of the programs we have included by clicking the "Next" button, or you can simply pick the topic that interests you by selecting the appropriate tab across the top. To stop the program at any time, just click the Exit button in the lower right-hand corner. Enjoy!

We have tried to make the GoodParents.com home page an excellent resource for up-to-date information regarding issues facing us as we try to help our kids while keeping them safe. At the site you will find monthly newsletters from me and a Parents Round Table where GoodParents from around the world will post situations that come up and ask advice from the rest of us on how best to handle them. You will also find valuable information on new products and services that we have reviewed and endorsed, new activities for your kids, and software libraries and interesting links for you.

You should find that the site is simple to explore and packed with helpful information. Of course, there is no charge for any of the information on the Web page.

Like all good Web sites, this one will be constantly changing. Check in once in a while at www.goodparents.com. If you use the ISP software that we have included and discuss in chapter 11, the site is already on your bookmark or "Favorites" list.

I hope to see you there.

Chapter Ten

∎

Installing and Using CYBERsitter™

I F YOU'RE NOT GOING TO use NetShield as your Internet Provider, you're going to want to at least use CYBERsitter. You've certainly read enough about CYBERsitter throughout this book. So let's go ahead and install it. This chapter will teach you all you need to know about this powerful program.

Once you install CYBERsitter, it will run all the time in the background of your computer. Whenever you or someone in your family goes on the Internet, CYBERsitter will know.

The team at Solid Oak software in Santa Barbara, California, has done a truly outstanding job on this program, integrating some of the most sophisticated technology in the world into an easy program for you to install and manage. Because you bought this book, you are entitled to a one-month free trial with no obligation. If school-age children will be using your computer to access the Internet, I *strongly urge* you to install this software. By the way, I don't strongly urge anything besides this, moving your computer to a public location, and taking a thirty-minute nap (parents, that is) at least once a day.

Once your trial period is over, CYBERsitter requires a one-time forty-dollar charge to keep the program running and up-to-date with the constantly changing Internet. It's really easy to upgrade and when you do, several extremely powerful features of the program are enabled. You'll want these, I promise, so you might want to think about pushing the "Register" button the first day. Like everything we recommend, if you're not happy with the product, just let us know and we'll make sure you get a full refund.

When you do register, I know that the program asks for your credit-card number and that you've probably heard terrible things about Internet security. Most of the things you have been told or read are just plain hogwash. In fact, the risks of loss on secure Internet transactions (transactions that are encrypted for safety) are so much hype that I personally guarantee that you will not lose a penny on this transaction. If you do, just drop me an e-mail at Robert.Maynard @goodparents.com and I'll personally ensure that you get your money back.

If you haven't already done so, put the GoodParents.com CD in your CD-Rom drive. The following screen will pop up after a few seconds, and there's my smiling face.

Click on the tab that says "CYBERsitter." Read a little description of what's going on and then just click on the CYBERsitter logo on the top of the window to launch the CYBERsitter Installer.

The CD will start whirring, snorting, coughing, and spitting. Eventually, you will see a window that looks a lot like this:

Click the "Next" key. You will see this warning.

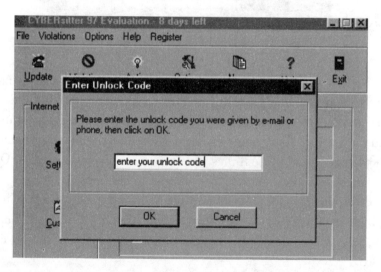

If you've tried another content-management product, hit the "Cancel" button and be sure to follow the instructions for that program to uninstall the earlier program. This is terribly important since these types of filtering programs don't like to interact with others of their same ilk. If you're not sure how to uninstall, contact the vendor of the program you are using now and they'll help you. Remember, if you use AOL, you can still use their parental controls and CYBERsitter will work just fine with it. CYBERsitter takes care of all the stuff out there on the Internet, and AOL takes care of the bad stuff inside their system.

Assuming that you are not using another program, or that you have successfully uninstalled anything you had before, from this point, click the "Next" button and we'll continue.

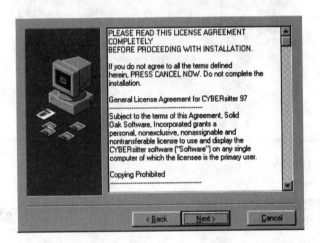

Now, you can go ahead and read all this, but basically what it says is that you won't attempt to make bootleg copies, that the software works, and so forth. I don't know anyone except software authors and the lawyers who charge exorbitant fees to write these agreements who actually read these things. If you think you should, read it. Once you are ready, click on the "Yes" button to continue.

Next, the installer program wants to know if you really want to install it. Instead of a "Next" button they should have a "Well, Duh" button. But, alas, they take themselves just a little too seriously. So . . . just click "Next."

In about a minute, you will see this screen.

Click on the "Finish" button and wait for your computer to shut down and restart. It's that easy!

When your computer restarts, you won't really see much of anything going on. This first time, you need to start the program manually to set it up. Look in the bottom left corner of your screen. See the "Start" button? Click it once. You will see a vertical list of selections appear. Roll the mouse up until "Programs" is highlighted in blue. Then roll the mouse to the right until you see Solid Oak highlighted, then click once on the CYBERsitter icon that pops up.

This will launch you to the CYBERsitter control panel. Because the Internet changes every single day, the first thing we need to do is

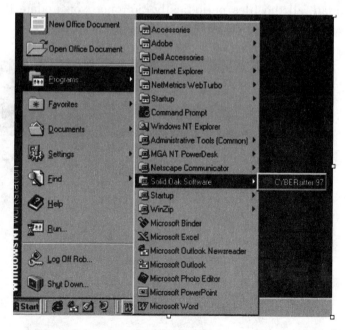

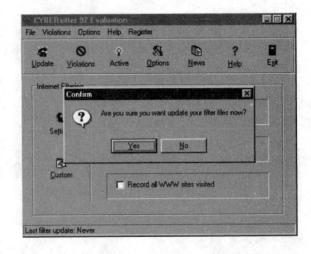

update the list of age-inappropriate sites that are out there. CYBERsitter makes this very easy.

And, unlike nearly every other piece of software that I've looked at, the publishers don't make you pay an annual fee to keep the list updated. Solid Oak, the maker of CYBERsitter, believes that once you pay for the software, you should actually get to use it without digging into your pocket every day.

To update the filter lists, click on the button that says "Update" and CYBERsitter will go out automatically and update the list once you confirm your wish by clicking on the "Yes" button. The version of CYBERsitter that we've installed for you will automatically go out and update all the files periodically. So, once you update the first time, you don't need to worry about it again.

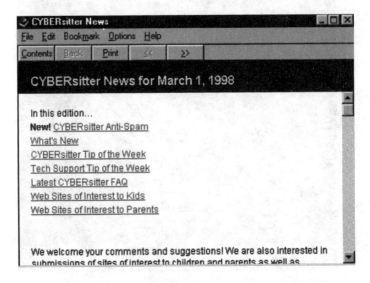

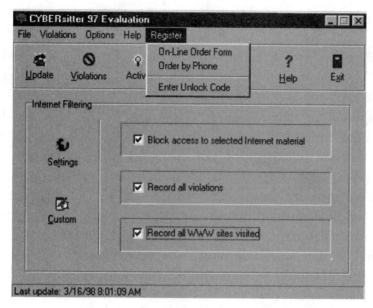

Once completed, you will see the CYBERsitter news screen—great stuff here published every month by Solid Oak. You can access this material any time by clicking the "News" button on the control panel. Once you're done perusing the newsletter, click on the little "X" in the upper right corner to return to the CYBERsitter control panel.

While we're talking about paying for the product, let me show you how. From the main CYBERsitter control screen, select the "Register" button, and scroll down to the "Online Order Form" like this:

Once you select the form, you should see this screen. If you don't use e-mail, you may want to select the "Order by Phone" option.

Fill out the information and select "OK" or talk to a Solid Oak sales rep. Either way, you will receive an "Unlock" code which you need to input to make sure CYBERsitter is running all the time. You enter this code by selecting the "Register" option on the main screen, then selecting the "Enter Unlock Code" option.

You can do this any time during the trial period and, once you do, you needn't worry about your kids running into anything that they shouldn't for as long as they use that specific computer.

To complete the setup, select the "Options" button. This rather formidable screen pops up. This is the heart and soul of CYBERsitter.

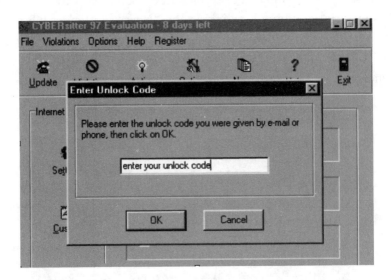

The first thing we want to do is keep the kids from the activities that have the highest risk factors. Personally, I keep my kids out of the newsgroups, the IRC systems, and File Transfer altogether. The web has excellent substitutes for IRC and Usenet that are much more

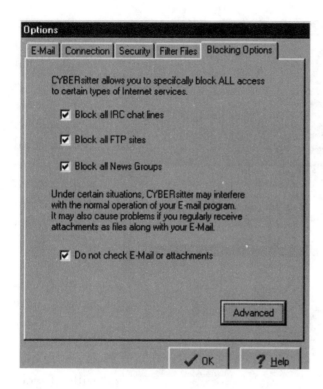

controlled. In case you skipped the rest of the book, you can find those alternatives in the News and Chat chapters (chapters 6 and 7) respectively.

File Transfer Protocol (FTP) is the best way to send and receive computer files, especially programs. Think of FTP as the equivalent of sex for your computer. At some point in every computer's life, it's necessary. It's also the easiest way to pick up or transmit a computer virus. So, you need to know who you FTP and, even if you know them, you should practice "Safe FTP." Until your kids come and ask for FTP access, just disallow it.

When they do finally ask for it, you need to have the facts-of-cyber-life talk. Reiterate the part of the Family Acceptable Use Policy that focuses on damaging or penetrating outside systems and make sure they know it is no joke to infect another computer system with a virus. Also, make them install a virus-protection program on your computer. Anything from Macafee, which produces virus-protection software, will be excellent. Don't worry, by the time your kids ask about this, they'll know how to get the virus-protection program and install it.

Once you have checked the appropriate boxes on the blocking tab, click the tab that says "Filter Files."

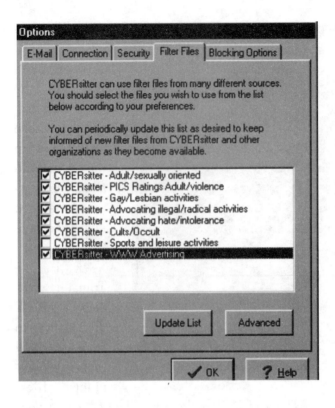

Select the subject headers that you think are inappropriate in your home. They're all pretty self-explanatory. When completed, select the "Security" tab. This is where you make sure that your kids can't disable CYBERsitter without your knowledge.

Enter a password that you will remember here.

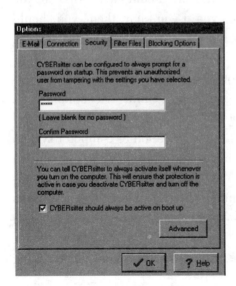

Take care when selecting your password. It needs to be something you can remember, but it shouldn't be something so easy that your kids can guess it.

A little trick that makes passwords a lot harder to break without making them harder to remember is to replace letters in a word with numbers that they resemble. For instance, my youngest daughter's name is Molly. If I were to use her name as a password, it would be pretty simple to guess. However, if I replaced the "o" in her name with a zero it would make it much more difficult for a casual hacker to break in. I could also replace one or both of the "l"s with the numeral "1." If I were to do this, the password would look like "m0lly," not so hard to remember, but much harder to hack. Try this trick in your password. Don't forget your password! You can't access the program without it.

You are now set up for CYBERsitter. Remember how we went to a search engine, entered "sex," and came back with a veritable smorgasbord of virtual carnality? Well, enter "sex" in any search engine now that CYBERsitter is running and you know what you'll get as a result? Nothing. *Sex* is one of the filtered phrases. Even when someone at your machine tries, the word is blocked from leaving your computer at all, so the search engine gets a blank query.

If you want to see what the kiddos are up to at any time, sit down at the computer and start CYBERsitter the way we did when we first set it up. Select the "Activity" button. Guess what? Plenty to talk about at dinner the next time . . .

Dates, times, who did it, how long they were online, and . . . see the "hotwire" entry toward the bottom . . . busted! The point here is

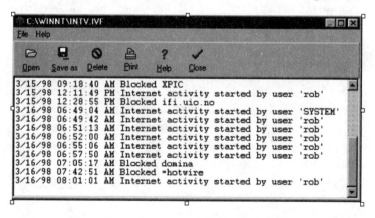

to tell the kids that you know what they're doing and you are perfectly capable of enforcing the rules of the house. You should get a much greater degree of cooperation and peace of mind with CYBERsitter running on the computer in your home.

Chapter Eleven

———————————■———————————

Installing Our Recommended ISP Software

S O YOU'RE READY TO TAKE the plunge and get your computer onto the Internet. Congratulations, you've made the right decision. Using the CD we've included to connect to one of our recommended ISPs will make your first trip onto the Internet as painless as possible.

Insert the CD that is included in the back of this book. Once you close the CD drawer, our program will start automatically and you will see this screen.

Select the tab across the top titled "Internet Install." You need to select whether you want filtered or unfiltered access to the Internet. If you aren't going to use the Internet much, or you aren't very comfortable around com-

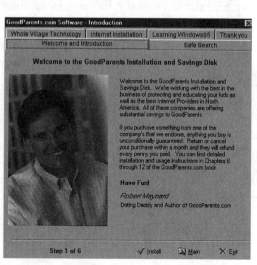

puters, you'll want to select filtered access through NetShield. If you want to sometimes see the seamier side of the Internet yourself, select unfiltered access. Both services cost exactly the same. It really is a matter of choice regarding the type of service that you are comfortable with in your home. All the services I recommend in this book offer unconditional satisfaction guarantees.

Make your selection by clicking on one of the radio buttons and then click "OK."

If you select filtered service, the install screens for NetShield come up. The artwork wasn't ready when I wrote this latest update, but it will be very straightforward and simple to install.

If you select unfiltered access, you will be installing some of the software from Mindspring. I think that Charles Brewer and his team at Mindspring have done the best job servicing their customers nationally. Their software is terrific and installs well.

After clicking on the "Unfiltered Access" button, you will see the Mindspring installation screen asking if you really want to install their software.

Click "Yes" and your CD will start spinning, your computer will start thinking, and eventually you will arrive at Mindspring's award-winning installation screen. Follow the simple directions and you'll be up and running on the Internet in no time. The software will automatically register you as a GoodParent and waive your installation fee and first month's service charge, saving you about forty-five dollars If you have any trouble, call Mindspring at (800) 719-4660 for help.

This program also asks for your credit-card number. I am so confident in this program that I will guarantee that you will not lose a penny on this transaction. If you do, just drop me an e-mail at Robert.Maynard@goodparents.com and I'll personally ensure that you get your money back.

Now that you're out there, check out our Web site at www.goodparents.com, let the kids roam from Yahooligans, and have a great time. If you haven't installed CYBERsitter, turn to chapter 10 and do it now. You won't regret it.